MARKETS AND MARKETPLACES OF BRITAIN

ANNA HALLETT

SHIRE PUBLICATIONS

Published in Great Britain in 2009 by Shire Publications Ltd, Midland House, West Way, Botley, Oxford OX2 0PH, United Kingdom.
443 Park Avenue South, New York, NY 10016, USA.

E-mail: shire@shirebooks.co.uk
www.shirebooks.co.uk

A CIP catalogue record for this book is available from the British Library.

Shire History no. 2 · ISBN-13: 978 0 7478 0689 9

Anna Hallett has asserted her right under the Copyright, Designs and Patents Act, 1988, to be identified as the author of this book.

Designed by Ken Vail Graphic Design, Cambridge, UK and typeset in Bembo.
Printed in Malta by Gutenberg Press Ltd.

08 09 10 11 12 10 9 8 7 6 5 4 3 2 1

COVER IMAGE

Cambridge Market Place, 1841, a watercolour by Frederick Mackenzie (1788–1854). (Fitzwilliam Museum, University of Cambridge/The Bridgeman Art Library)

PAGE 2 IMAGE

'The Scottish Market Place', 1818; oil on canvas, attributed to Sir David Wilkie (1785–1841). (Wolverhampton Art Gallery/The Bridgeman Art Library.)

NOTE ON PRE-DECIMAL CURRENCY

In this book, historical prices are stated in the old, pre-decimal currency. Before February 1971, when the present decimal system (£1 = 100p) was introduced, the United Kingdom currency comprised the pound sterling (£), consisting of 20 shillings (s.), each of 12 (old) pence (d). There were thus 240 old pence in the pound. Thus one shilling equals 5 new pence, and one old penny approximately equals 0.4 of a new penny. The value of the pound remained the same. Old prices were written, for example, £12 18s. 5d, or sometimes £12/18/5 (that is, 12 pounds, 18 shillings and 5 pence). Inflation has reduced the purchasing power of the currency, so that quoting a decimal 'conversion' for a sum of the old money is not useful.

DEDICATION

For Ruud and Josepha: in admiration.

Shire Publications is supporting the Woodland Trust, the UK's leading woodland conservation charity, by funding the dedication of trees.

CONTENTS

INTRODUCTION

> SATTURDAY was their biggest Market day … which is like a faire for all sorts of provision and goods and very cheape: I saw one buy a quarter of lamb for 8 pence and 2 pence a piece good large poultry; here is leather, woollen and linnen and all sorts of stands for baubles…

(Celia Fiennes on visiting Newcastle-upon-Tyne in 1698)

MARKETS developed when self-sufficiency gave way to specialisation, when hunter-gatherers settled down in permanent communities in which the various tasks needed to sustain the population came to be divided amongst people who each concentrated on a particular skill. Farmers, potters, toolmakers, leatherworkers and other craftsmen all produced more goods than they needed for their own use, thereby creating a surplus which they would hope to exchange for commodities made by others. To facilitate this process, people soon agreed to meet at a certain time in a space specifically allocated for these transactions. It has been suggested by some that prehistoric stone circles may have had a trading function as well as a religious or astronomical one. (English Heritage mentions this possibility for Castlerigg in Cumbria.) After all, large gatherings of people, who may have travelled some distance, provide commercial opportunities.

The resulting markets attracted not only local people but also traders from further afield. Across Britain trade routes were developed, and tracks dating to prehistoric times can still be found where for centuries people have travelled in each other's footsteps. Specific products such as flints from East Anglia, salt from Nantwich (Cheshire) and Droitwich (Worcestershire), pottery from Peterborough and stone tools from Wales and Cornwall have been found in places far from the areas of production or extraction. For example, axes that could be traced to the Graig Llwyd quarry in North Wales have been discovered between Warwick and Coventry.

In *c.* 200 BC sword-shaped iron currency bars came into use as a means of exchange in southern England, where examples have been found on Hayling Island (Hampshire). By *c.* 150 BC these were being superseded by coins, and specimens dating from this early period have been discovered in Portchester and Horndean (both in Hampshire).

In time the marketplace became the centre of a community, an open space not only used for the buying and selling of goods on a regular basis, but often also the seat of local government and justice, visibly present in the shape of a moot hall, guildhall, town hall, or – in Scotland and the north of England – a tolbooth, usually incorporating a court and cells, with a pillory and stocks and a weigh-beam (or tron in Scotland) close by. This was the place for public punishment and execution. With the introduction of Christianity, a parish church might be built close by and a market cross erected, serving as a focal point for traders and as a place where public announcements or political statements could be made. In a period when most streets were unpaved, the marketplace might be cobbled over as a sign of its importance. (In 1385 Great Yarmouth in Norfolk was proud to record that its marketplace was partly paved.) Often a pump or conduit provided a very important amenity at a time when most households did not have a private water supply.

OPPOSITE
Dairy cattle for sale in Buckingham Market Square in 1935. Hurdles have been placed by the roadside to prevent cattle from entering the houses. The building on the right is the Old Gaol, now a museum. (By kind permission of the Museum of English Rural Life, Reading University.)

Equally a sundial, in later times joined or replaced by a clock, might be situated here. And, because of its central position, the marketplace was – and often still is – the site of commemorative features such as statues, sculptures, plaques and inscriptions.

Predominantly an urban feature, a marketplace was regarded as a sign of prosperity and superiority – a status symbol. It has been described as 'one of the truest expressions of a town's identity', setting it apart from the rural village. Where the latter was primarily concerned with agricultural matters, the market town was about prosperity through trade in a money economy, serving not only the inhabitants but also those living in the countryside surrounding it. And when on market days a town came alive, as it still may do, it was not just its traders who did business: shopkeepers, publicans and those offering professional services, such as auctioneers, accountants and lawyers, all benefited. Thomas Hardy's description of his fictitious town of Casterbridge (based on Dorchester in Dorset) as 'the pole, focus, or nerve-knot' of the surrounding country life would have fitted most market towns.

The importance of markets is shown in the number of place-names that include the words 'market' or 'chipping' (*ceap* is Old English for 'market' or 'marketplace'). Examples are Market Harborough and Market Bosworth in Leicestershire; Market Brough and Hesket Newmarket in Cumbria; Market Drayton in Shropshire; Downham Market and Thorpe Market in Norfolk; Wickham Market, Newmarket, Stowmarket, Needham Market and Market Weston in Suffolk; Market Rasen, Market Stainton and Market Deeping in Lincolnshire; Market Overton in Rutland; Market Warsop in Nottinghamshire; Market Weighton in Yorkshire; and Market Lavington

BELOW
Many public events took place in the market square. A Review in a Market Place, c. *1790; pen and ink with watercolour on paper, by Thomas Rowlandson (1756–1827). (Yale Center for British Art, Paul Mellon Collection, USA/The Bridgeman Art Library.)*

in Wiltshire. In Essex we find Chipping Hill and Chipping Ongar; in Gloucestershire Chipping Sodbury and Chipping Campden; in Oxfordshire Chipping Norton; in Northamptonshire Chipping Warden; and the counties of Lancashire and Hertfordshire each contain a settlement called Chipping. In Dorset Blandford Forum adopted the Latin term for 'marketplace' (*forum*).

Though this book is mainly concerned with the trading activities for which the marketplace was developed, the importance of this area as a centre for a community in so many other ways must not be forgotten. It also has to be remembered that usually a charter would grant a town the right to hold fairs as well as markets. Whereas the latter usually happened weekly, as they often still do – bringing local traders with everyday regional produce for sale – fairs, generally tying in with a saint's feast day, would last for several days and take place once, twice or maybe three times a year. On these rarer occasions merchants dealing in more exotic goods would come from far and wide, probably bringing itinerant quacks and tooth-pullers in tow, as well as those providing entertainment, an element that survives in the form of funfairs.

ABOVE *The fourteenth-century cross, restored in 1878, in Lydney (Gloucestershire).*

BELOW *A selection of street signs including 'Market'.*

Chapter One

THE DEVELOPMENT OF MARKETS

THE ROMANS, whose successful conquest of Britain began in AD 43, introduced the concept of towns to the country and founded a considerable number of these near Celtic strongholds, developing their efficient road system often following existing prehistoric tracks. Along these they founded trading posts at strategic points. An example of this can be traced in Warwickshire, where Alcester, Mancetter and Cestersover were linked in such a way.

Roman cities were built to a standard pattern and usually included a marketplace – the forum – at the intersection of the two main streets, the *decumanus* and the *cardo*. Here the main temple and the principal administrative centre and court of justice – the basilica – could be found (a pattern not very different from the later marketplace with parish church and town hall). When Chichester (Sussex) lost its importance as a military site the Romans founded a small town with a marketplace within the area of the present city, then situated in the kingdom of the Atrebates, a Celtic tribe. They called it Noviomagus ('new market'). In Wroxeter (Shropshire) the archaeological remains of a market destroyed by fire sometime between AD 165 and 185 have been unearthed, providing evidence for the kind of commodities offered for sale there at that time. As stalls were knocked over, with traders fleeing the scene in a panic, the owner of one of these had to leave behind his stock of Samian ware (red pottery with a bright glossy surface, made in central Gaul and the Moselle valley) – now on display in the Shrewsbury Museum and Art Gallery. Here also the special provisions market, or *macellum*, could be found, just as in other Roman cities.

As the Romans withdrew from Britain, in the early fifth century AD, their place was taken by invading Germanic tribes, including Angles, Saxons and Jutes. These essentially rural people at first mostly ignored the abandoned cities and founded their own trading settlements, often along the rivers that formed their main transport system, at busy crossroads and river fords, as well as near natural harbours. Even though road-building declined, some major Saxon highways, like those following the lines of the present A1 and A38, were maintained as important routes connecting strings of flourishing trading posts.

On the south coast, one of these, Hamtun, developed not far from its Roman predecessor, Bitterne, and both now form part of Southampton (Hampshire). Derby developed where major routes came together as they crossed the River Derwent. Ipswich (Suffolk), which considers itself to be the oldest continuously settled Anglo-Saxon town in England, was founded near a crossing point on the River Orwell, on a site for which there is archaeological evidence of Stone Age and Roman occupation. Melton Mowbray (Leicestershire) was developed in Saxon times in a place where a number of prehistoric tracks came together, crossing the River Wreake.

OPPOSITE
Market Morning, Birmingham, 1876. J. Drake, in The Picture of Birmingham *(1831), describes how in the Bull Ring different areas were 'by common consent appropriated to the sale of different articles' with even 'the causeways attached to the churchyard filled with small dealers … with exhibitions of books, stationery, white mice, and singing birds', as well as 'large parterres of crockery ware'. (The Bridgeman Art Library)*

The Cross in Chester, dating to 1407, marks the centre of the Roman town, where the two main roads, the decumanus *and the* cardo*, crossed.*

Another example is Braintree (Essex), which grew up at the crossing of two pre-Roman tracks. Post-Roman settlements often contain traces of earlier street patterns within the remnants of ancient boundary lines (which can include parts of former walls, ramparts and gateways), indicating that later occupants of the site were happy to absorb these features into their own town plans. In Chester the medieval marketplace came to be situated at the junction of the two roads that in Roman times had led to the four gateways of the town.

Into these early settlements farmers from the neighbourhood brought their surplus crops, and there merchants from further afield offered goods and services not locally available. In February 1982 the grave of an itinerant Anglo-Saxon smith was discovered at Tattersall Thorpe (Lincolnshire); the grave contained an impressive array of tools, quantities of iron, copper alloy and lead, small amounts of silver, flecks of gold and bits of scrap (now on display in The Collection, the museum of art and archaeology in Lincoln), which have been dated to the second half of the seventh century. The owner of this unique set of tools and materials may well have been travelling from market to market, hoping for trade.

As money was not at everyone's disposal in the early days, many market transactions would have been in the form of barter, with goods changing hands without coins being used. However, as time went on, currency became important and for that reason mints were established, usually in market towns, where the need for coins was most obvious. There are many examples of this, including Canterbury (Kent), Norwich (Norfolk), Derby, Lincoln, Nottingham, Leicester, Tamworth (Staffordshire) and York.

Because in the Saxon period many markets came into being spontaneously, in response to local need, it is often difficult to trace their early history – to know when and how they started. Many of the most successful and long-established markets were held by prescriptive right, that is by custom, without an official licence, some maybe going back as far as Roman times. An example is Berwick-upon-Tweed in Northumberland, where a market existing in this early period may have continued right up to 1124, when the town received its charter.

CHARTERS

In time a charter might be obtained from the local landowner or, more often, the king, for whom it was a source of income, as the privilege had to be paid for. This formalised the customary arrangement by setting out the rights and duties of those profiting from the now officially established amenity. The charter received by Peter de Bermingham in 1166 from King Henry II allowed him and his heirs to have a 'market on Thursday at his castle of Birmingeham with thol and theam [the right to charge tolls] and soc and sac [the right to hold a local court] and infangenethef [the right to bring to justice any thief caught within the lord's jurisdiction in possession of stolen property]'. In 1257 Henry III granted Baldwin de Insula and his heirs 'certain specific weekly markets … at his manor of Huniton [Honiton], co. Devon'. Also in the thirteenth century, the same king gave Corfe Castle (Dorset) borough status and granted it a market on Thursday. However, here no charter was received until in 1576 Queen Elizabeth I issued letters patent confirming the rights of the landowners and citizens of Purbeck. Another example is Adam Nowell, lord of the manor of Netherton, Great Harwood (Lancashire), who was granted the privilege of holding a weekly market on Thursdays by Edward III.

Though many markets were founded in the centuries after the Norman Conquest, others came about later, maybe after an increase in the local population, bringing with it business opportunities for those willing to serve new customers. In eighteenth-century Derbyshire, the rapid expansion of the lead-mining community of Winster led to the grant of a market to Thomas Eyre of Rowtor, allowing him 'one market upon Saturday each week forever for buying and selling all manner of goods and cattle and Beasts … with all tolls and profits to the markets … pertaining'.

Of great benefit was the fact that a charter made it difficult for rival markets to be developed within a certain distance, as stipulated in the document. New markets were not normally allowed nearer than 6⅔ miles from an established one. The distance between markets was held to be an average day's journey for anyone wanting to buy or sell and then return home. The thirteenth-century English jurist Henry of Bracton explained that 'an ordinary day's walk may be taken at twenty miles, and dividing the time into three portions, the morning will be used going to market, the middle of the day in buying and selling, and the other third part of the time in returning home'. However, a charter given by King James VI of Scotland (later James I of England) to Stranraer (Dumfries and Galloway) in 1596 stated that no other market was to be held within the 'space of four myles in circuit'.

There are quite a few examples of new markets endangering the viability of existing ones. In the twelfth century Woodbridge (Suffolk) successfully petitioned Henry II for a market charter in the face of strong opposition from Ipswich traders. When the town of Watton in Norfolk received its market charter from King John there was a challenge from the neighbouring parish of Saham Toney, then a royal manor and of greater importance than Watton, whose market, however, triumphed. This was greatly resented and feelings remained high for centuries, with violence breaking out in 1375. Some say the matter has still not been forgotten. In Devon, William Brewer, who had been granted the manor of Axminster in 1220, said that the market there was being damaged by the markets of Sidmouth (Devon) and Lyme Regis (Dorset), and in Wiltshire the new market established in 1219 at Salisbury damaged the older one at Wilton.

Salisbury market (Wiltshire) with the fifteenth-century Poultry Cross. A nineteenth-century view.

Sometimes unfair competition was the result of delinquent behaviour: in 1382 the Bishop of Coventry and Lichfield was accused of having held a market in Rugeley (Staffordshire) for twenty years without a licence from the king and to the prejudice of the burgesses of Stafford, who were losing 12d per year as a result. The rule covering rival markets continued to be implemented so that, when in 1813 an Act of Parliament allowed naval commissioners to 'establish a market at the town of Pembroke Dock', a payment of £3,000 was required in compensation for the fact that it would be competing with the ancient market at Pembroke.

There were also always strict instructions regarding the day of the week on which the market could be held, a rule that even now applies as the stipulations of earlier charters are still adhered to. The reason for this was again to stop unfair competition or, as was stated in the charter granted to Morpeth (Northumberland) in 1199, 'so … they be not to the nuisance of neighbouring fairs and neighbouring markets'. (Even so, the nearby and superior settlement of Mitford saw its market and fair decline as Morpeth built a bridge over the River Wansbeck for easier access.) In 1203 Lichfield (Staffordshire) was fined for changing its market day from Sunday to Friday. In 1220 in Devon Faulkes de Breaute complained that the prior of Sidmouth had changed the day of the market from Saturday to Sunday, without the king's licence, to the detriment of neighbouring markets – hereby possibly trying to protect his own market at Honiton. When in 1560 Queen Elizabeth I renewed the charter of Hartland (Devon), she confirmed that the market should be kept for 'the whole day of Saturday, so that the … market … be not to the prejudice of other neighbouring … markets'. Buckingham's charter of 1554, granted by Queen Mary I (against a payment of 'twenty shillings, at the Feast of St Michael the Archangel'), also warned that the market should not be 'to the Hurt of neighbour Markets'.

Sometimes a town requested a change of market day, to avoid competition. This happened in nineteenth-century Wantage (Oxfordshire), where, after a successful petition, the market was moved from Saturday, as laid down in the charter, to Wednesday. In this way it overcame rivalry from Reading (Berkshire), with the result that the corn trade as well as the general market improved. For travelling traders it was helpful to be able to sell goods in different towns on different days, as they do to this day. An additional benefit of a charter was exemption from the tolls and taxes that itinerant salesmen had to pay, giving resident dealers the advantage of being able to keep their prices low.

The charter given to 'Lewis Pollard, Esquire, Robert Carey, Esquire, William Abbott, Esquire, Hugh Stuckle and Hugh Purst, Gentlemen and their heirs and assigns' of 'Harteland in the County of Devon' by Queen Elizabeth I, allowing them to hold two fairs annually and 'one market on every Saturday in every week … for Cattle, Merchandises and all other things there to be bought and sold forever to be held and kept during the whole day of Saturday…' (By kind permission of Stephen Hobbs and Hartland Town Council)

Amongst the towns receiving early (Saxon) charters were Shrewsbury (Shropshire) in 901, Derby in 917, Nottingham in 918, Lincoln in 924 and Chester in 939. Both Shepton Mallet (Somerset) and Canterbury (Kent) had a market charter by the eighth century and Oundle (Northamptonshire) obtained one in 972. The Domesday survey, drawn up for William the Conqueror in 1086 to provide him with details of all the lands in England, mentions just fifty markets, though almost certainly there were more. Amongst them are Clare (Suffolk), described as 'then as now a market', Frome (Somerset), Tutbury (Staffordshire) and Cirencester (Gloucestershire). Abingdon (Oxfordshire) is represented as having 'ten traders at the gates of the abbey' and Melton Mowbray, the only place in Leicestershire indicated in this way, is listed as controlled by Geoffrey de Wirce at a return of 20s per annum. In Norfolk Downham Market was confirmed as a market before the Conquest and flourished until it was overtaken by King's Lynn and Swaffham in the same county and by Wisbech (Cambridgeshire).

Between 1100 and 1200 about eighty new market towns were established by landowners keen to improve their income. Particularly on poor soil, the rents, tolls and fines paid by citizens and visiting traders generally amounted to a great deal more than any crops or livestock on the same plot could provide. A number of these towns were planted by the monarch, on land owned by him. During the following 150 years another two thousand new markets were founded, some in what at first were no more than rural communities, each governed by a charter. At the end of the thirteenth century Edward I established a network of castles in Wales, each with its own privileged borough. Here only English traders were allowed to operate, as at Aberystwyth (Ceredigion). Welshmen were prohibited from holding a market within 10 miles of these towns, so Machynlleth (Powys), approximately 19 miles north of Aberystwyth, was developed as a Welsh market.

Not all markets succeeded, mainly because they were unable to attract trade. This might lead to a slow fading away or to the landlord deciding to revert the land to agricultural use. The now quiet village of Haughley (Suffolk) was a market town from 1231, when Henry III granted it a charter, to the eighteenth century, holding its market on the now empty green. (The Old Counting House pub, a fourteenth-century timber-framed building overlooking the former marketplace, may well have been used by traders to pay their dues.) In Warwickshire the village of Cestersover received its market charter in the early fourteenth century, only to be destroyed by its owner, Henry Waver, so that the land could be used for pasture. The village of Stottesdon (Shropshire) was an important place in Saxon times and the seat of local government. In the thirteenth century it received a charter allowing it a market and fair, but it was overshadowed by nearby Bridgnorth and Cleobury Mortimer and so never made it as a town.

By 1066 the right to establish a market was regarded as a royal franchise but it was only from the thirteenth century onwards that the king insisted on this right. From 1199 royal grants were recorded in the Charter Rolls, listing details such as the name

Haughley Green (Suffolk), where once a market was held. The Old Counting House pub (now a restaurant), facing it, may have been the tolsey, where market dues were paid.

The charter given to Tiverton (Devon) by Oliver Cromwell in 1655 at the request of the citizens, who sought permission to change their market day from Monday to Tuesday to avoid displeasing God by setting up their stalls on Sunday. (Courtesy of Tiverton Town Council)

of the person to whom it was given, the day of the week on which the market could be held and its location in the town. From the reign of King John (1199–1216) the ruler further asserted his right to issue a new charter should any changes be requested regarding the timing, duration or location of an existing market. In 1655 the local authorities of Tiverton (Devon) petitioned Oliver Cromwell to be allowed to change the town's market day from Monday to Tuesday because it was believed that the floods and fires it had recently suffered were God's punishment for setting up the market on a Sunday night.

The granting of charters became a regular source of income for the monarch. For example, in 1201 the citizens of Hartlepool (Durham) paid King John 30 marks (one mark was the equivalent of approximately 66p) for theirs. At first this legal fee was not too onerous. However, after an outbreak of the Black Death in 1348, with fewer

King John signs the charter given to Stafford on 1 May 1206. Though the sum to be paid for this privilege is not mentioned, 'dues and ancient fee farm rents' had to be paid into 'our Exchequer by their own hands … to wit – one moiety at the feast of the Passover and the other at the Feast of St Michael'. This stained glass window is situated above the Market Square entrance to the Guildhall shopping centre, erected in 1953. (By kind permission of Danny Pickard.)

citizens left to pay tax, at a time when Edward III was already short of money, the king decided that a periodic renewal of charters, against payment of course, could be the answer to his problem. So, for example, in 1349 he withdrew Huntingdon's charter of 1205, changed it slightly, and returned it against a lump sum. Then in 1364, when funds were needed for the war against the French, the same thing happened again. This reissuing of charters now became a regular occurrence, with market towns expecting to pay renewal fees from time to time. Hereford received its first charter from Richard I in 1189. This was renewed twice by Henry III, in 1227 and 1256, and subsequently six more times up to and including the reign of William and Mary. Sometimes readjustments had to be made to cope with changed circumstances. In Hawkshead (Cumbria) King James I granted the farmers of the area the right to hold a market in the town because they had been deprived of the one they had used at Furness Abbey when this was destroyed at the dissolution of the monasteries. A charter granted by King Charles II to Tring (Hertfordshire) stipulated that during the Friday markets the morning should be devoted to trading straw plait (an important industry in the area) and the afternoon to corn.

THE MARKETPLACE

With the introduction of Christianity, churches were erected in most settlements, usually facing the central trading area or marketplace, where these were already in existence. This arrangement was generally adhered to in the later, planned towns. Often one of the few permanent buildings in a community, the church became a focal point for public activities, trading amongst them. The setting up of market stalls in church buildings or the surrounding churchyard is frequently mentioned in documents. (In this context it has to be remembered that a church had the nature of

Plan of sixteenth-century Birmingham, based on Bickley and Hill's plan of the town in 1553. The triangular marketplace is shown close to 'The Manor Place' and St Martin's parish church. Here the market cross, Corn Cheaping and shambles are clearly shown. The 'Tole Booth is located between the High Street and English Market which leads to Welch Market'. Birmingham already had an important livestock market by the mid thirteenth century. The west–east route through the town was used by increasing numbers of cattle drovers from Wales and the north of England. A drover's licence, a brass badge stating 'Drover 12', can be found in the Bull Ring Gallery, Birmingham Museum and Art Gallery. (By kind permission of Joseph McKenna.)

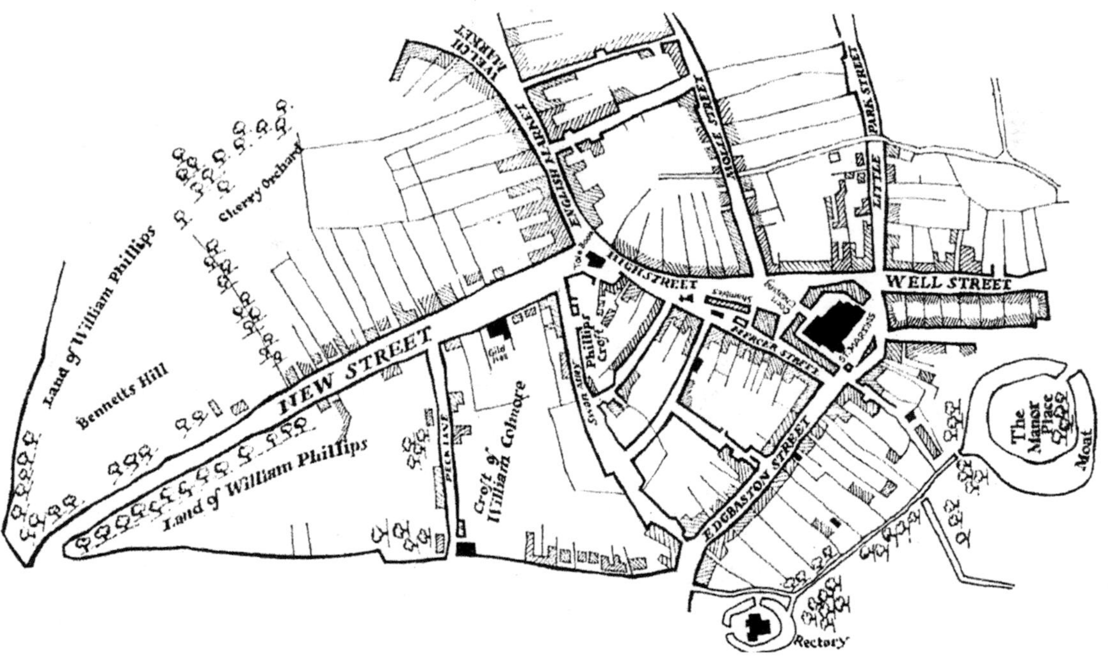

a community building, with the chancel, for which the priest was responsible, used for religious purposes, whilst the nave, in the physical care of the parishioners, could be used for secular activities, including trade and the sealing of business deals.) Churches and churchyards were seen as places of safety and protection as one would not expect to be cheated or attacked on consecrated ground. In Reepham (Norfolk) the marketplace was once the churchyard where the three manors of Hackford, Whitwell and Reepham met, each building its own church there.

However, in 1268 the Papal Legate issued instructions forbidding the setting out of stalls for merchandise within the walls of the church. This was followed by a statute of Edward I, issued in 1285, which stated: 'And the King demandeth and forbiddeth that from henceforth neither fairs nor markets be kept in Churchyards, for the honour of the Church.' Even so, it took many years for this custom to die out everywhere in the country. In 1390 St Peter's Church in Barnstaple (Devon) set up six stalls in the churchyard which were allocated to 'divers men at a rent of twenty shillings', in addition to the stalls owned by the church in the High Street, 'let to divers men for the sale of fish and meat'. Right into the sixteenth century the Monday markets in Much Wenlock (Shropshire) were held in the streets and churchyard. In the same period traders in Woodbridge (Suffolk) used the churchyard to avoid paying rent.

Marketplaces differ in shape and size, depending on the circumstances prevailing at the time of their development. Some grew spontaneously and irregularly, perhaps at a junction of major roads or by a ford or bridge across a river. Others were planned, as part of a new town or newly developed area in an existing settlement. Triangular marketplaces often came about where three main routes joined up, as at Carlisle (Cumbria), Market Harborough (Leicestershire), Bampton (Oxfordshire), Taunton

Market Street, Haddington (East Lothian).

(Somerset), Richmond (Yorkshire) and Birmingham. In Alnwick (Northumberland) the three-sided marketplace (now partly built on) was formed where an ancient track split in order to go in two different directions. In some cases irregularity came about as the result of a market being imposed by the lord of the manor (once he had obtained his charter) on an established settlement which would have involved the demolition of some buildings, to make way for the new amenity, whilst others might be left standing to be accommodated in the revised plan.

Rectangular marketplaces may be the outcome of four roads meeting or an indication that it was planned as part of a rectilinear street plan, as in Salisbury (Wiltshire), Lichfield (Staffordshire) and Londonderry (or Derry) in Northern Ireland. (In Derry the importance of the market to local people is illustrated by the fact that in the mid nineteenth century a permanent breach was made in the city wall, to accommodate an extra route, Newmarket Street, to the market in the centrally located Diamond or Square.)

Some market places were linear, maybe widening out along a particular stretch to accommodate market stalls in the bulge of the resulting cigar shape. These usually occurred along a town's main thoroughfare. Examples include Chipping Campden (Gloucestershire), Henley-in-Arden (Warwickshire), Haddington (East Lothian) and Crail (Fife), where the lengthy Marketgate was known as one of the largest marketplaces in medieval Europe. Sometimes a town improved its situation by diverting a major road into its market area. This was achieved in Thame (Oxfordshire), where the Bishop of Lincoln re-routed the road from Aylesbury (Buckinghamshire) through the town, in Dunster (Somerset) and in Boroughbridge (Yorkshire), where the Great North Road was redirected in this way. In Kimbolton (Cambridgeshire) Geoffrey Fitzpiers re-routed the main street through the marketplace in 1200. Some marketplaces were extremely large, to accommodate the huge numbers of cattle and sheep regularly sold there. Examples of this can be found in St Ives (Cambridgeshire), Cirencester (Gloucestershire) and King's Lynn (Norfolk).

BELOW LEFT
The Buttermarket in Canterbury (Kent) is situated outside Christ Church Gate leading to the cathedral.

BELOW RIGHT
The spacious marketplace in front of the gatehohuse leading to the ruins of Battle Abbey (Sussex), dedicated to St Martin, and founded by William the Conqueror after his defeat of King Harold in 1066.

The Market Place with market cross situated between the two main streets leading to the castle after which Corfe Castle (Dorset) has been named.

Many markets developed spontaneously, or were founded, in front of monasteries, convents and cathedrals – institutions offering protection and trading opportunities in return for the market dues paid by those merchants who rented stalls on their land. A Saxon example is the long open market established by the monks of St Augustine's Abbey, situated outside the wall of Canterbury, in the street called Longport. Another early one was founded in St Albans (Hertfordshire), where, according to the *Gesta Abbatum* (the medieval records of the abbots), the tenth-century Abbot Wulsin established a market outside the abbey gate. In Tavistock (Devon) the market developed outside the Benedictine abbey which was founded there in 981, and in St Ives (Cambridgeshire) a market came into being in 1290 in front of St Ivo's Priory. In Canterbury an area now called the Buttermarket occupies the site in front of Christ Church Gate leading to the cathedral (which until its dissolution during the Reformation included a monastery, now in ruins). In Evesham (Worcestershire) the substantial market square is located just outside the Norman gate belonging to the former St Mary's Abbey. Other examples can be found in Spalding (Lincolnshire), where a Benedictine priory lay to the south of the present marketplace, and in Battle (Sussex), where the spacious market area is situated just outside the imposing gatehouse to the abbey founded by William the Conqueror in thanksgiving for his victory over King Harold here in 1066. Kelso (Scottish Borders) claims to have the largest marketplace (now called The Square) in Scotland, which can be found just outside the ruins of its former abbey, dedicated to the Blessed Virgin and St John. The marketplace of Melrose (Scottish Borders) was established close to the Cistercian abbey founded there in 1146.

Marketplace, Peterborough. A nineteenth-century view.

For reasons similar to those given for the development of marketplaces outside ecclesiastical establishments, trading areas were established in front of castles and other strongholds. Here towns often grew up in response to the business opportunities afforded by the initial building project, followed by the continued maintenance of the structures and the needs of those living and working in them. Under the protection of the castle, a thriving market would provide an excellent source of income to both traders and the castle owner. In Scotland, Edinburgh is a prime example and the towns of Selkirk (Scottish Borders) and Dumbarton (West Dunbartonshire) also developed around the marketplaces that had been established outside the gates of their respective castles. In Wales Caernarfon (Gwynedd), Carmarthen, Montgomery (Powys) and Llandovery (Carmarthenshire) show a similar picture, and in England Windsor (Berkshire), Bristol, Launceston (Cornwall), Dudley (West Midlands), Richmond (Yorkshire) and Woodstock (Oxfordshire) provide further evidence. At Kilpeck (Herefordshire) a market was formerly held in what is now a grassy area in front of the castle mound and Norman church famous for its carvings. In Corfe Castle (Dorset) the Market Place is situated between the two main streets forming a V shape as they run towards the castle.

Some towns developed more than one market within their boundaries. The reasons for this were various. In Coventry the town was divided between the prior and the earl, each part with its own market area – the former triangular in shape, the latter occupying part of the High Street. In Lichfield (Staffordshire) the reduction of market space in the centre caused by the construction of St Mary's Church led to the creation of a second trading site in the area known as Greenhill. In King's Lynn (Norfolk) the earlier Saturday Market, established in 1101 by Bishop Herbert de Losinga of Norwich, was supplemented by the sizeable Tuesday Market in the area called Newland, developed to the north of the original town by Bishop Turbe in 1140. Beverley (Yorkshire) added the large Saturday Market to its earlier Wednesday Market, which had grown up close to the Minster. Very conveniently, the names of these latter markets indicate the day of the week on which trading took place – and generally still does. In Penzance (Cornwall) the original meaning of the name 'Market Jew Street' ('Jew' is a bastardisation of the word *diyew* or *diew*, meaning 'second', 'other' or 'Thursday') points to the possibility of more than one market area. As we shall see, in many towns, including Canterbury (where the area called Wincheap, outside the former city wall, is a reminder of this), there were markets in many areas of the urban settlement.

Sometimes a market was moved to a different part of the town, as circumstances changed. This happened in Pontefract (Yorkshire), where a more spacious site was found away from the castle, where it had first developed. Other examples include Bury St Edmunds (Suffolk), Denbigh and Peterborough. In Norwich the Saxon market, situated in the area known as Tombland (meaning 'open space'), was replaced by the present marketplace in Norman times, to make way for the cathedral and its close. In Bridport (Dorset) the Saxon marketplace south of the parish church of St Mary was abandoned for a later one at the junction of South Street

Market Place, Wisbech (Cambridgeshire). The market moved here in the twelfth century from its original site, now called Old Market, on the other side of the River Nene.

with West Street and East Street. Wisbech (Cambridgeshire) moved its commercial centre across the River Nene from Old Market to the present Market Place in the twelfth century. In Ludlow (Shropshire) it has been estimated that an early market was situated along the bulge of Corve Street – originally the most important through road. With the construction of the castle and Dinham Bridge across the River Teme just behind it, a new route came into existence, causing the area in front of the castle to develop into the present marketplace. At Brough (Cumbria) an early planned settlement at the foot of its castle (now known as Church Brough) lost out against the later one of Market Brough, established nearby at the junction of two trade routes.

Within a marketplace merchants generally grouped together according to the products they sold. Fruit and vegetables could be found in the green market – in Carlisle (Cumbria) this is the name of an area close to the town hall – and dealers in dairy produce might be allocated the north side of the market square because it was considered to be the coolest. Corn merchants occupied yet another part of the market. In Banbury (Oxfordshire) Cornhill leads off the Market Place. A similar situation can be found in Penrith (Cumbria), where the area named Cornmarket is set back from the Market Place, forming an L shape. This town also had a wheat market, a market for horses and pigs and one for oats and pease. In Lichfield (Staffordshire) the Cloth Cheaping was on the south side of the Market Place, the Women's Cheaping (later Breadmarket Street) on the west side, the Salt Market on the north side and Butchers' Row on the east side. The swine market was in nearby Tamworth Street. These divisions might be observed over the centuries so that even in nineteenth-century Romford (Essex) the eastern end of the market was used for cattle and pigs and the western end for farm tools, clothing, fruit and vegetables.

In some cases surrounding streets might be taken over by traders, their names still indicating what commodity was for sale there. Very close to the main square of Kelso (Scottish Borders) can be found Wood Market, Horse Market and Coal Market. In Shrewsbury, at one time by far the most important market in Shropshire, Butcher Row, Fish Street and Milk Street are similarly close to the centre. In Perth, Salt Vennel

The Haymarket, Norwich, 1825; oil on panel, by David Hodgson (1798–1864). (Yale Center for British Art, Paul Mellon Collection, USA, /The Bridgeman Art Library.)

View of the Lawnmarket, Edinburgh, by William Gavin Herdman (1805–82). (City of Edinburgh Museums and art Galleries / Bridgeman Art Library.

is a reminder of the former salt market there. Pontefract (Yorkshire) has streets called Horse Fair, Woolmarket, Shoemarket and Cornmarket. There is a Swine Market in Kirkby Lonsdale (Cumbria) as well as a Horse Market, and a Meal Market in Hexham (Northumberland). Rye (Sussex) has Fishmarket Street and in Newcastle-upon-Tyne there is Bigg (a type of barley) Market. In Penzance (Cornwall) Bread Street and Wood Street are located near the Market Place, as is the earlier mentioned Market Jew Street. In Norwich (Norfolk) can be found Timber Hill as well as Cattlemarket Street. In 1698 Celia Fiennes described the situation in this town as follows:

> the Hay market which is on a hill a very steep descent all well pitch'd as before, this comes to another space for a market to sell hoggs in; one runs along behind, which is all for stalls for the Country butchers that bring their meate for the supply of the town, which pay such a rent for them to the town ... by it is a large market for fish which are all at a little distance from the heart of the City so is not annoy'd with them, there is a very large Market place and Hall and Cross for fruite and little things every day, and also a place under pillars for the Corn market.

Somewhat later Daniel Defoe wrote: 'The markets in Edinburgh are not in the open street, except that in the high street, where there is every morning an herb and fruit market, which yet abates before noon, and what remains then is no grievance. Besides this, there are several distinctive market places wall'd in, and reserv'd for the particular things they are appointed for, and very well regulated by the magistrates, and well supplied also.' He then listed: 'The Meal-Market', 'The Flesh-Market', 'The Poultry-Market', 'The Butter-Market', 'The Grass-Market' and 'The Horse Market' – the two last 'kept open, and in the same street just within the West Port, with several others. There is also, in the street call'd the Land-market, a weekly market for all sorts of woollen manufactures, and some mercery and drapery goods, and also for linnen cloth.'

Edinburgh still has its Grassmarket and Lawnmarket, with Fleshmarket Close and Old Fishmarket Close, coming off High Street. In 1783 William Hutton said of Birmingham: 'For want of a convenient place where the sellers may be collected in one point, they are scattered into various parts of the town. Corn is sold by sample in the Bull Ring ... the beast market is kept in Dale End, that for pigs, sheep and horses in New Street ... if a man hath an article to sell which another wants to buy, they will quickly find each other out'. Sometimes different goods were sold on different days of the week. In Scarborough (Yorkshire) pots, earthenware and glass goods were sold on Thursdays in Newborough (a main thoroughfare), whereas a general market was held on Saturdays in Princess Street.

Butchers' Row, Coventry from the North End, *by S. R. Lines (1804–33). (Maidstone Museum and Art Gallery/The Bridgeman Art Library.)*

The amount of meat consumed by English people was often commented on by foreign visitors and this predilection provided a source of income for many butchers, as well as farmers. Local husbandmen not only bred animals for the market but might also provide a final resting place where livestock brought in by drovers over long distances from the north of Scotland, Wales and even Ireland could be fattened up.

Butchers, as well as fishmongers, were often allocated a space that was slightly away from the main market area because of the mess they generated. Butchery has always been an untidy business. Nowadays much of the unpleasant side is done away from the public eye, but in medieval times animals were slaughtered in the street, with all the noise and pollution (in the form of blood and offal) that this activity brought with it. Butchers' stalls came to be known as 'shambles' (a term deriving from the Anglo-Saxon *fleshammels*, or 'flesh shelves', which eventually was used for extreme untidiness in a more general way). Occasionally the name 'fish shambles' is used in documents.

MEAT AND FISH MARKETS OR SHAMBLES

Early town plans often indicate where the shambles or meat market was situated. The most famous example is the much-photographed street of that name in York. A map of Birmingham, dated 1553, names a long narrow building in the market area (known as the Bull Ring) as 'Shambles'. In Hereford the Old House Museum in High Town is the only surviving part of the row of houses that was once known as Butchers' Row, built in 1621. M. D. Lobel's map of 1800, describing this area as 'Butchery', shows it to have been a little distance from the main market. A similar map for Salisbury, also dating to 1800, shows 'Butcher Row', a street that still exists (as does Fish Row), also near the marketplace. In Bradford-on-Avon (Wiltshire) the narrow, pedestrianised 'Shambles' is located a short distance from the site of the medieval market, and in Bristol a widening of Old Market Street (site of the first suburban market of the city, possibly dating to the twelfth century) indicates the place formerly occupied by the shambles. In 1546 the town authorities of Great Yarmouth (Norfolk) erected a large building for the butchers, to which in 1551 a slaughterhouse was attached. All meat had to be sold there and anyone disobeying was fined. The shambles of Leeds could be found in the middle of the main street, Briggate, and, together with the Moot Hall next to it, were considered an obstruction until they were removed in 1825. In Kingsbridge (Devon) the building formerly occupied by the butchers, and still known as The Shambles, is now used as a café. The arches of the seventeenth-century shambles in the marketplace of Settle (Yorkshire) have been filled in and made into shops. Bewdley (Worcestershire) has

Drovers' route near Llanwrtyd Wells, Powys.

ABOVE
Stroud (Gloucestershire): Shambles Market near the church still has the wooden counters which are propped up on market days but when not in use rest against the wall under the awning.

ABOVE LEFT
The fifteenth-century shambles in Shepton Mallet (Somerset), 'a very rare and lucky survival' according to Sir Nikolaus Pevsner.

turned its eighteenth-century shambles into a museum. The Shambles in Wetherby (Yorkshire) were built by the Duke of Devonshire in 1811 and let by him at 3 guineas (£3 3s.) per annum. However, in 1888 the building was converted into an open market for poultry and dairy produce. Butchers' Row in Barnstaple (Devon) is situated opposite the Pannier Market and consists of a row of one-storey butchers' shops, of which there were thirty-three when first built. (The butchers were given a permanent building in 1714, long before dealers in other commodities were housed in the Pannier Market, in 1855.)

The town hall in Bridport (Dorset), erected in 1786, originally accommodated butchers' stalls on the ground floor under the open arches. In 2007 meat was still one of the commodities available there. The former shambles in the marketplace of Hexham (Northumberland), dating to 1766, consist of an open building with Tuscan columns on three sides and wooden posts completing the remaining side. In Stroud (Gloucestershire) the shambles were developed by John Bond, butcher, when he leased the market and two cottages in 1651. Here John Wesley preached from a

The town hall, Bridport (Dorset). Built in 1786, it originally had butchers' shops on the ground floor under the open arches. In 2007 a butcher's shop inside still continued the tradition.

butcher's block in 1742. Situated close to the parish church, it is still a busy market. Two of the original shelves survive, attached to a wall and protected by an awning, and are propped up on market days to form counters. Slightly away from the main market area of Shepton Mallet (Somerset) stand the fifteenth-century shambles, described in the Pevsner Architectural Guide to North Somerset as a 'wooden shed' and 'a very rare and lucky survival'. Behind the arches of the splendid nineteenth-century Market House at Castle Cary (Somerset), in its own yard, the worn though still sturdy shambles were brought back into use in 2008. The low benches are situated on a platform and have a drainage channel underneath.

The general nuisance of meat markets was often commented on. The custom of slaughtering and bleeding animals in Glasgow's Trongate, which went on till the end of the seventeenth century, was described as a 'verie loathsome practice'. In 1714 the inhabitants of Morpeth (Northumberland) petitioned Lord Carlisle, the lord of the manor, to have the 'Shambells … Erected in a more convenient place they being at present very inconvenient and a Great Nusance to the Publicke Markett where they now stand'. In early seventeenth-century Totnes (Devon) the butchers of the Flesh Shambles were told that they must leave 'noe bloud, garble or skulles within the towne to annoye the people'. In Perth the shore porters were expected to 'cleng and dycht [clean]' the market. The early nineteenth-century butchers of Southwell (Nottinghamshire) were asked not to kill their animals on the street or throw 'sheeps bags or gutts or any other nastiness' into the marketplace. In Kendal (Cumbria) the 'Old Shambles' in front of the 'Beast Market' were replaced by the 'New Shambles' in 1804. Twelve butchers' shops were built along an ancient path, Watt Lane, situated on a slope that allowed the blood and offal to flow towards the river. There were no drains leading down from any of the many slaughterhouses around the marketplace and even though the owners paid 2s. 6d per week for the lane to be cleaned the New Shambles soon came to be known as 'Stinking Lane'.

When in 1820 the chapter of Southwell Cathedral decided to rebuild the Crown inn, which until then had had butchers' stalls underneath, it decided not to allow 'the trade or business of slaughterman, butcher, tallow chandler or melter of tallow, … or any other trade apparently injurious or offensive to the neighbourhood without special license'. In Rye (Sussex) the butchers' stalls in Market Street were very close to the architecturally interesting public water house or cistern, and in 1754 mention was made of the several calves' feet that were found there. However, whereas in seventeenth-century Clare (Suffolk) butchers were forbidden to slaughter openly in the street because they caused pollution by throwing away their 'paunches and offall', in Perth animals had to be killed in full view of prospective buyers. In most towns the area where the shambles were located not only became encumbered with heaps of evil-smelling offal, but also with dunghills resulting from the many animals up for sale or waiting to be slaughtered.

New Shambles, Kendal (Cumbria): twelve butchers' shops built in 1804. Their location on a sloping site was meant to help with the removal of blood and offal down to the river. However, it soon became known as 'Stinking Lane'.

So it is not surprising that over time local authorities tried to impose order on a trade that was notoriously undisciplined. Barnstaple (Devon) appointed a 'Keeper of the Shambells', who, on taking office, took an oath (probably dating to the seventeenth century) promising 'truly to see the trestles and boards safely to be set forth to them that shall bring flesh or fish to this Town and market and to see the Trestles and Boards safely to be kept and all belonging to my power. Soe help me God.'

Many towns had fish markets, particularly along the coast. Inland it was more difficult and far more expensive to buy this commodity in a fresh state. Fast horsemen called 'rippiers' supplied traders away from the sea with saltwater fish, but at a price that made it a luxury. In Lewes (Sussex) fishwives (known as 'juggs') brought their pack donkeys from Brighton along Juggs Lane and Newmarket Hill. Fish sold in Tunbridge Wells (Kent) came from Hastings (Sussex). In Canterbury (Kent) the fish shambles were in Burgate, near the church, with fresh supplies coming in from Whitstable. Freshwater fish came from rivers and lakes. In the twelfth century King John granted Pooley Bridge (Cumbria), situated on Ullswater, a charter allowing the town to hold a fish market for the char (a deep-water fish) that was brought ashore here in great quantities.

Dalton-in-Furness and Cartmel (both in Cumbria) have fish slabs. Though no longer in use, the stone platform and pump at Cartmel form an interesting feature in the centre of the little town. Just as was the case with meat shambles, complaints were made about the mess created by fishmongers. In early seventeenth-century Totnes (Devon) these traders were forbidden to cast 'eny gutts, ffish or ffilth under their stalls'.

MARKET STALLS AND ENCROACHMENT

Pictorial records clearly illustrate the different ways in which merchants displayed their goods. Many of the larger traders used trestle tables, with or without a roof or awning, such as are still found in most markets today. Smaller traders, maybe farmers' wives, might spread their wares out on the ground or arranged in baskets. The previously mentioned medieval shambles in Shepton Mallet (Somerset) are not so different from later booths. A nineteenth-century description of the market in Great Yarmouth (Norfolk) describes 'a spectacle full of interest with long rows of stalls stretching from end to end. You pass from peas and potatoes, mushrooms as large as dinner plates, very fine raspberries and other fruits and vegetables to a display of

The Fish Slabs, Cartmel (Cumbria). Locally, the Market Square is referred to as the 'Market Cross and Fish Slabs', even though the original cross has long gone.

Old Market, Warrington (Cheshire), 1877.

meat and poultry not to be seen elsewhere. There are baskets, bedding, boxes, shoes, frippery, old iron and new hardware and second hand books. A knife grinder and a cheap jack with his crockery next to hassocks, cushions, matting and horse collars made from the rushes with which the broads abound.'

In 1722 Elizabeth Derrett paid £1 as six months' rent for the 'butter women's stool' in Stroud (Gloucestershire). However, there were those who tried to avoid paying market tolls, with some traders trying to hawk their wares in the streets or from house to house. Others, with the same aim in mind, set up their own stalls rather than pay for the official ones provided. In King's Lynn (Norfolk) the butchers, in particular, were often troublesome in this way. In 1661 there were twenty-two butchers' stalls in the Saturday Market Place and thirty in the Tuesday Market Place, yet still meat sellers set up their own booths, even after a decree of 1667 stated that this was not allowed unless the official shambles were full.

Over time some of the temporary stalls, which should have been taken down and stored between market days, took on a more lasting nature and they became permanent buildings (recognisable today by the fact that they do not have gardens). In this way built-up areas within the marketplace were created, diminishing the overall open space. This infill happened in many towns and examples can be found in different parts of the country. In Ludlow (Shropshire) the island of houses created in this way was divided into three blocks by narrow lanes, each of which came to be occupied by members of a particular occupation: drapers, butchers and shoemakers. In the same town two further 'islands' occupy the area of the Bull Ring. In the nineteenth century one of these was known as 'The Shelds', a corruption of the Latin *selda*, meaning 'stalls'. In Lichfield (Staffordshire) the market originally developed all round St Mary's Church. However, by the beginning of the sixteenth century the area on the south side of the marketplace started to be permanently occupied. This encroachment later continued on the east side.

Similar infill can be found in Ashby-de-la-Zouch (Leicestershire), Chippenham (Wiltshire), Beverley (Yorkshire), Eye (Suffolk), Saffron Walden (Essex),

Market Place, Monmouth, 1877. In 1724 the Shire Hall was built on the site of the Elizabethan market hall. Under its open arches it provided space for traders dealing in corn, flour, wool and hops. The Court of Assizes was held on the first floor.

Ludlow Market Square, *watercolour by Louise J. Rayner (1832–1924). (Haynes Fine Art/The Bridgeman Art Library)*

Thame (Oxfordshire), Stow-on-the-Wold (Gloucestershire) and Perth, as well as in many other places. Sometimes encroachment has led to a great reduction of the market area. In Aylsham (Norfolk) the nineteenth-century town hall is situated near the centre of the original trading area, blocking a large part of the earlier open space. In High Wycombe (Buckinghamshire) the medieval marketplace stretched from the Guildhall to the top of Frogmoor, where the initial width of the whole area, later partly filled in with streets, can be observed. In Denbigh an island block encroaching on the marketplace created the enclosures of Crown Square and Back Row, severely curtailing the original market area. Equally the former marketplace situated between the castle, church and Guildhall in Windsor (Berkshire) is now almost completely covered by shops along the narrow lanes of Market Street, Church Street and Church Lane. In seventeenth-century Wymondham (Norfolk) the infill of Market Hill with shops, as planned by the lord of the manor, did not take place after his tenants

Market infill, Thame (Oxfordshire). There has been a market here since 1230. Between the Buttermarket on the cooler, north side and the Cornmarket on the south side temporary stalls eventually gave way to more permanent buildings.

petitioned him to leave things as they were. Sir Henry Hobart seems to have agreed with the argument put forward that covering the market area would have been 'an exceedinge great blemishe both to the [market] Crosse & markets place', leaving 'no standings for cattell, nor convenient place for people to walke in'.

LIVESTOCK MARKETS

The livestock market was very important in many towns, as it allowed farmers to buy and sell cattle, sheep and pigs. These would be tied to rings embedded in the walls of nearby buildings – tethering rings can still be found in Deddington (Oxfordshire), Malmesbury (Wiltshire) and Winchcombe (Gloucestershire) – or exposed in temporary pens made out of timber hurdles. St Ives (Cambridgeshire) still has its hurdle house, the building in which the panels were stored when not in use, though it no longer serves its original purpose. In Ottery St Mary (Devon) the hurdles were kept in a building that doubled as the local lock-up. Fodder for the animals brought to market was stored in nearby buildings. In Malmesbury redundant haylofts can be seen in the houses surrounding the former cattle market, now a car park. In Kirkby Lonsdale (Cumbria) fodder was kept behind a low-gated arch on the corner of Swine Market and Horse Market. Usually animals of the same kind were grouped together in particular areas of the market or town. In Bromyard (Herefordshire) the High Street from the Falcon to the top of the town was known as the Beast Market, Cruxwell and Old Road were called Sheep Street, and Rowberry Street is the later name of Swine Street. In Deddington (Oxfordshire) pigs were sold in the centre of the market, sheep in the Bull Ring and horses in Horsefair.

BULL RINGS

Many towns have areas in or near the marketplace called the Bull Ring. Here bulls would be tied up, either to be displayed for sale away from other cattle, or for the purpose of baiting (by dogs) – as a sport, or to improve the quality of the

The marketplace at Wymondham (Norfolk) with the market cross dating from 1617–18, replacing an earlier structure destroyed by fire.

meat the slaughtered animal would provide. An early statute stated that bulls for slaughter and human consumption should be baited, as it softened the carcass. This rule is reflected in a seventeenth-century by-law in Hereford that obliged butchers to bait all bulls before they were killed in order to tenderise the meat. In 1746 in Appleby-in-Westmorland (Cumbria) one John Orton of Kirkby Stephen (Cumbria), butcher, was fined 3s. 4d for exposing 'bull beef, not baited'. (In the same town in 1772 John Shepherd and Joseph Nelson were fined 13s 4d 'for baiting a bull about the hour of three o'clock in the morning'.) Sometimes a bull might escape and cause damage. In Alnwick (Northumberland) an angry bull attacked two tradesmen, one of whom broke a leg and was wounded in the head.

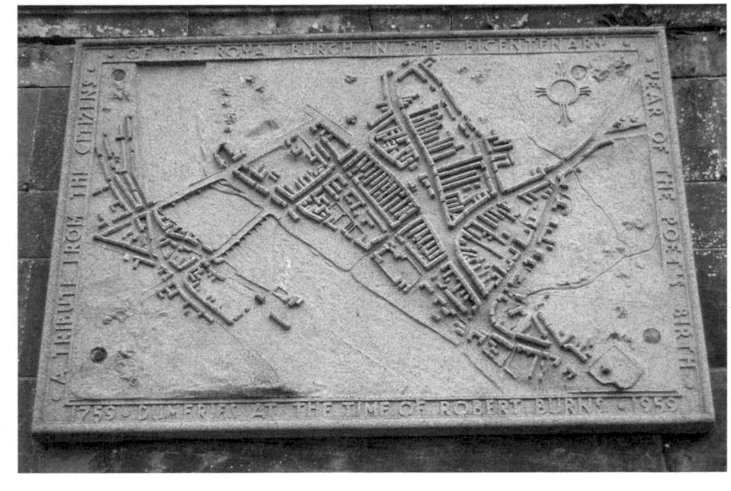

Town plan of Dumfries, showing market infill (attached to the midsteeple in the high street).

Bulls would be tied to a ring in the pavement (examples can be found at Kelso in the Scottish Borders and at Appleby-in-Westmorland in Cumbria) or to a stake or stone. In Morpeth (Northumberland) the rope with which the bull was attached to 'a great stone' was kept in the council chamber at the town hall, whilst the shoemakers looked after the bulldogs used for the baiting. It was said that 'ladies from the country came to Morpeth and sat in the windows of the Market Place to witness the bull baits, like the Spanish women'. In Totnes (Devon) the bull ring dug up in the Plains is now on display in the Guildhall. In Darlaston (West Midlands) the Bull Stake, which is still in evidence, was always regarded as the centre of the town. In Canterbury (Kent) the area now called the Buttermarket was formerly known as the Bull Stake. Here the most expensive apartments to rent in the fourteenth-century 'White Bull' faced the baiting area.

Tethering ring, Horse Fair, Deddington (Oxfordshire).

Of the many areas known as bull rings in Britain one of the best known is the one in Birmingham, first mentioned in 1553. Other examples can be found in Ludlow and Much Wenlock (both in Shropshire), Llantrisant (Rhondda Cynon Taff), Skipton (Yorkshire) and in Cullompton (Devon), where there is a Higher Bull Ring and a Lower Bull Ring. In Kirkby Stephen a ring of cobblestones gives an outline of the former bull ring, which was used till 1820, when the escape of a bull put a stop to further baiting.

Bull ring in the centre of Market Square, Kelso (Scottish Borders).

HORSE MARKETS

Until cars and other motorised vehicles took over, horses provided the fastest form of transport. There were millions of these animals in Britain, used on the land, for the carriage of goods and for travel. As a result, many places had markets where a wide range of horses could be bought and sold – animals for riding, hunting, pulling carriages and carts or farm implements such as ploughs, and for use in the army and, later, the police. Usually horses were allocated to a particular area in the market, though sometimes the trade was given a separate marketplace of its own. Often there was room for horses to be put through their paces, as at Deddington (Oxfordshire), for a buyer needed to see the animal gallop in order to be able to judge its quality – in contrast to cattle, which were considered for their meat.

The importance of the horse trade is reflected in the street names that still remind us of this. Amongst the many examples are Birmingham, Kidderminster (Worcestershire), Hinckley (Leicestershire), Deddington (Oxfordshire), Rugeley (Staffordshire), Bristol, Pontefract (Yorkshire), Romsey (Hampshire), Wetherby (Yorkshire) and Wisbech (Cambridgeshire), all with 'Horse Fairs' or 'Horsefairs'. Kelso (Scottish Borders), Barnard Castle and Darlington (both in Durham), Oswestry (Shropshire) and Kirkby Lonsdale (Cumbria) have areas called 'Horse Market', and Leicester has a Horsemarket Street. As happened with other livestock, horses driven through town could cause problems and on market days people often tried to protect their properties from damage. Maybe Rampant Horse Street (named after a thirteenth-century inn) in Norwich and the alleyway called Rampant Horse Lane in Downham Market (both in Norfolk) are reminders of misbehaving animals.

The strict rules prevailing in Clare (Suffolk) meant that sales had to be witnessed by a third party, at the conclusion of which the crier would announce the outcome of the transaction, as is shown in the following example:

'18 December 1617. Memorandum … that one John Cope of Tuddington in the County of Bedford, husbandman, did bargaine and openly sell for v li. Ijs. and viijd.

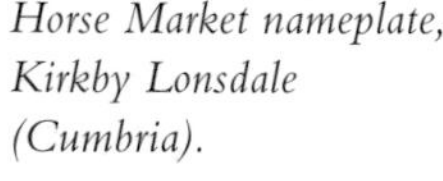

Horse Market nameplate, Kirkby Lonsdale (Cumbria).

Unto one Thomas fflacke of Stansfeilde in the countye of Suff. In the open market of Clare ... One trotting cot of the age of two yeares and a half, of an Irone Gray collor, and yt was verified by the testimonye of on John Woman of Tuddington aforesaid, husbandman, that the said John Cope was true owner of the said colt, in the presence of Wm. Constable, Peter Farmer (Bailiffs).'

Fair dealing always remained important, as is shown by the rules stated in an auction catalogue, dated 4 March 1911, for the South Shropshire and Central Wales Horse Repository in Craven Arms (Shropshire). Dealers were warned that 'Horses described as "good workers", "having been worked", "used to farm work", "quiet in all gears", "suitable for town work", or other description in the opinion of the Auctioneers calculated to convey the impression that the horses were capable of reasonable work, shall constitute a warranty that the same are quiet and capable of working'. Also 'A SHIVERER cannot be classed as a good worker, or sold as sound. A CRIB-BITER, WIND-SUCKER OR RIG must be so described in the catalogue. A SHIVERER costing 20 guineas or over is returnable unless stated at the time of the sale.'

Horse sales were often concluded in pubs, the time-honoured place for the sealing of market deals as well as for other types of business. In Newtown (Powys) the Buck inn was used for this purpose and in Chester the Boot inn in the Rows has an original horse-trader's seat in the back room, though without the curtains it once possessed.

Horses need constant feeding, just as cars need refuelling, and hay markets were the equivalent of today's petrol stations. Most towns had an area where animal fodder was for sale and street names still remind of this. Examples can be found in London, Leicester, Basingstoke (Hampshire), Newcastle-upon-Tyne, Tunstall (Staffordshire) and Norwich. Hay is a bulky commodity, requiring substantial space for storage. This was another trade that was regarded as messy because inevitably strands of dried grass would be lost in transport and, caught by the wind, deposited over the area surrounding the market.

The Moot Hall in Aldeburgh (Suffolk) dates from c. 1520–40. Here the town council still meets in the main chamber upstairs. Originally it had an open market area and prison cells at ground level. The seat in the south wall (behind the street sign) is said to have been put there to give periodic rests to people in the stocks.

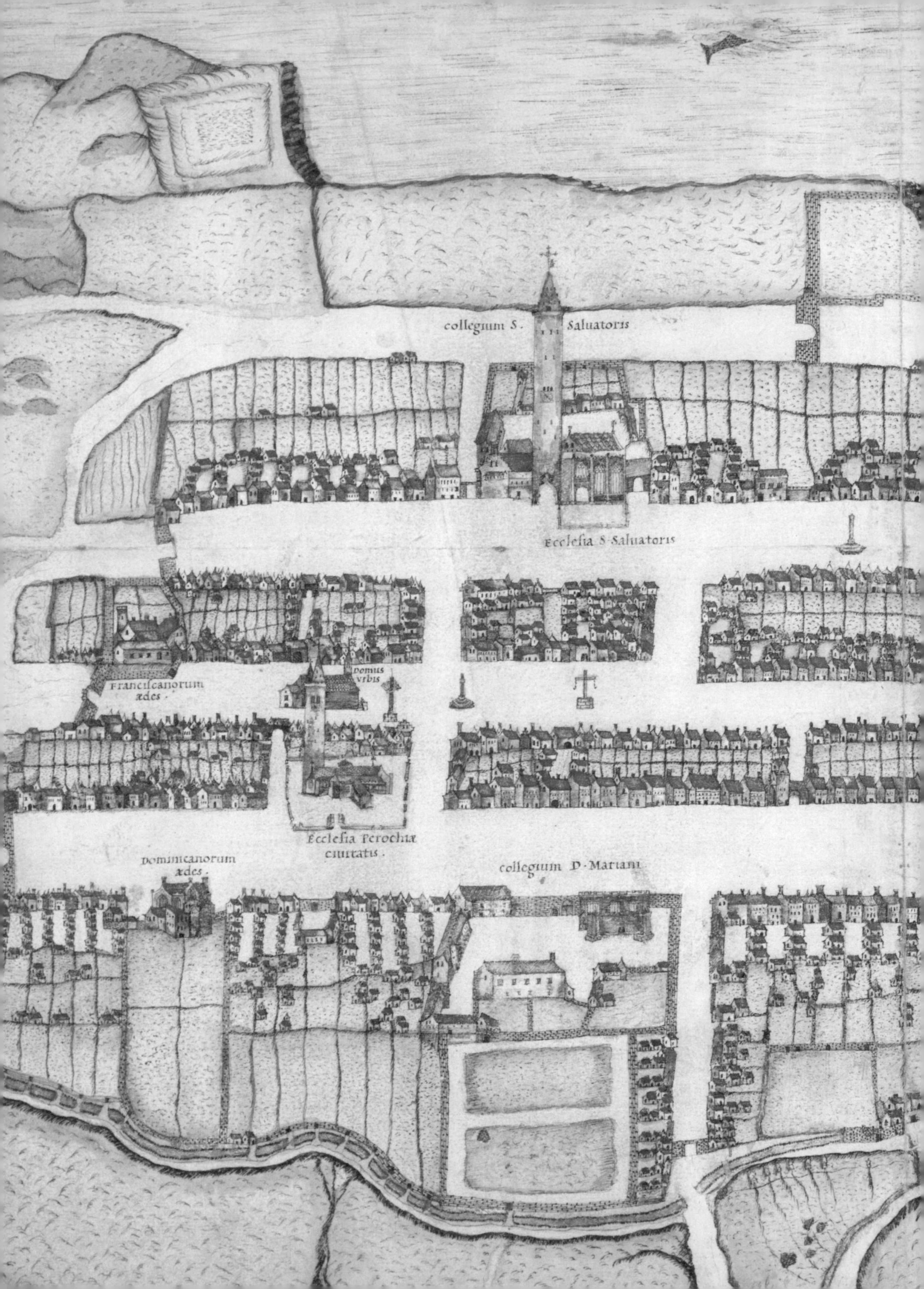
collegium S. Saluatoris
Ecclesia S. Saluatoris
Franciscanorum ædes.
Domus Vrbis
Ecclesia Perochiæ ciuitatis.
Dominicanorum ædes.
collegium D. Mariani

Chapter Two

THE MANAGEMENT OF MARKETS

RULES AND REGULATIONS

THERE have always been market rules, including stipulations regarding the day or days of the week on which traders can operate, opening and closing hours, the size of stalls to be used, and the fees or tolls to be paid. Also the merchandise must be of good quality. Medieval regulations were numerous and complicated, and many of them were concerned with fairness in dealing, hoping to protect traders from harmful competition and consumers from high prices and sharp practice.

As we have already seen, it was important that a town's market day or days did not clash with those of neighbouring towns. From Saxon times onwards many markets were held on Sundays, providing traders with a captive group of customers who came from the surrounding area, as well as from the town itself, to attend mass, and who in turn found it convenient to be able to stock up on necessities without having to travel a second time in the week. When William the Conqueror founded the abbey of St Martin in Battle (Sussex) he granted a regular Sunday market as a source of income for this new religious body. The twelfth-century market charter received by the Benedictine monks of Eynsham (Oxfordshire) allowed two annual fairs to be held, as well as a market on Sundays and Tuesdays. In thirteenth-century Scotland King Robert de Bruce gave the town of Crail (Fife) permission to hold Sunday markets in Marketgate. Equally, the charter received by Stranraer (Dumfries and Galloway) said that the town should have its market on Sundays.

However, the practice came to be frowned on as incompatible with religious observation and an English statute dating to the thirteenth century ordained that it should stop – a rule that was not always obeyed. This was long before the same prohibition came into force in Scotland, as a result of the Reformation. An Act passed by the Scottish Parliament in 1579 forbade all sabbath markets and fairs throughout Scotland. In Crail those not obeying were 'prohibited from repeating the offence under pain of exclusion and debarring themselves, their wives, bairns and servants from all benefit of the kirk in the time coming, viz: Baptisms, the Lord's Supper, and Marriage'. So the market was transferred to Saturday, but people kept breaking the rules and in 1607 a new Act was passed, changing the market day from Saturday to Friday. We have already seen that the citizens of Tiverton in Devon petitioned Oliver Cromwell to allow the town to change its market day from Monday to Tuesday in order to put a stop to the setting up of stalls on the sabbath. This seems to suggest that by this time most people were convinced that anything relating to Sunday trading was wrong. However, Romsey (Hampshire) waited till 1826 before it changed its market day from Sunday to Thursday.

OPPOSITE
St Andrews (Fife) from the south, c. 1580, showing the tolbooth 'domus urbis', *pillory, mercat cross and tron. (By kind permission of the National Library of Scotland.)*

Market bell, St Nicholas Market, Bristol.

A town's charter not only laid down the day or days of the week on which a market could be kept, but also stipulated where it could take place and what its duration was to be. An Act of 1350 made it compulsory to mark the opening and closing of a market by the ringing of a bell. In Alnwick (Northumberland) no man could buy or sell before the bell tolled eleven o'clock, whilst in Morpeth (Northumberland) traders had to wait until the bells of St Mary's Church sounded nine o'clock. In Barnstaple (Devon) the Guildhall bell was used for the same purpose. The reason for this rule was the prevention of 'forestalling'. This meant going out before the market had started and buying from those who would otherwise have brought the goods to market themselves, in order to resell at a higher price. Another rule stated that 'engrossing' – buying up the whole or a large part of the stock of a particular commodity, and selling it for an enhanced price – was not allowed; nor was 'regrating', the buying of goods in one market for resale in another. A further statute was directed against the 'badger', defined in an attestation of 1500 as 'such as bryngeth whete to towne, as wele in trowys, or otherwise, by lande and by watir', in other words an itinerant dealer who acted as a middleman, and whose dealings were considered dishonest if unlicensed. One of the rules in Broughton-in-Furness (Cumbria), mentioned in its charter, forbids buying or selling 'in corners, backsides or hidden places'.

The main objective was to keep prices low. An Act of 1533 gave certain members of the Privy Council the right to set 'reasonable' prices for 'cheese, butter, capons, hens, chickens and other victuals necessary for man's sustenance'. To make sure the various rules were obeyed, it was important that all transactions took place out in the open, in the marketplace. Forestalling and regrating were seen as ways of evading price control. Furthermore, these practices would lead to a loss of income on the part of the owner of the market, who could charge toll on certain goods in the market as well as taxes on the stalls set up there. In sixteenth-century King's Lynn fishermen were often accused of dealing with Dutchmen and other 'strangers', in attempts at forestalling and regrating. An undated document, possibly belonging to the twelfth or thirteenth century, found in a cupboard at All Saints' Church in Helmsley (Yorkshire), directs those who had to ensure that traders behaved fairly to 'Inquire of forestallers, regraters and engrossers of corn, victuals and other goods, for the first offence imprisonment for two months and the loss of the value of the thing sold, for the second offence imprisonment for half a year and the loss of double the value of the goods and for the third offence imprisonment during the king's pleasure and judgement of the pillory and forfeiture of the goods and chattels'.

Even though a statute of 1772 repealed the bans on forestalling, regrating and engrossing, it seems that these practices continued to be frowned on right into the nineteenth century. In late eighteenth-century Lichfield (Staffordshire) people from outside the town were not allowed to buy until one hour after the opening of the market at 11 a.m.; in this way it was hoped to prevent the buying of products to sell elsewhere. In 1847 an article in a Devon newspaper described the following incident taking place in Honiton: 'On Saturday a little dealer intercepted a load of potatoes which were being brought for sale in the market and bought the whole load up at 1/6 a score and then immediately began to retail them at 2/3. The women, however, interfered and would not allow him to do so. They opened the bags and threw the potatoes about the streets, and eventually the man yielded, and sold them all at 1/6.'

The same article relates two cases of engrossing. The first one concerned a farmer bringing a lot of wheat to town and selling it to a dealer, who was about to remove it. But the people would not let it go and the seller was forced to retail it to the poor at 12s a bushel. The second one told of a load of flour that had been lodged at the Golden Lion for some person at Ottery St Mary, who was removing it in his wagon when the horses, 'being spirited, trotted off pretty fast with their load. One of the sacks of flour fell off and burst and the people got hold of it.' However, the mayor and his council did not agree with this kind of behaviour and after an extraordinary meeting 'convened for the adoption of special measures to preserve the peace – a great number of the inhabitants were sworn in as special constables and a notice issued by the mayor for the purpose of reassuring the farmers and others frequenting the market'.

Some rules related to health and hygiene. In 1692 the magistrates of Stranraer (Dumfries and Galloway) reported that 'a weekly flesh mercat' was held 'on the first day of November to the first day of January and no longer' for the 'common good'. Orders covering the nineteenth-century market building in Bath (Somerset) included: 'No unwholesome meat, fish or vegetables shall be exposed or brought into the market; no person shall curse, swear or make use of threatening or abusive, obscene or disgusting language in the market; no boys shall play or saunter in the market, nor shall any person lounge or sit on the standings or stalls; all skins shall be removed from the butchers' market by nine o'clock in the morning; no person shall throw or fling vegetables, garbage or any missile in the market.'

In Birmingham only a certain number of hawkers were allowed in the Bull Ring market and those wishing to sell in this way had to apply for a licence on a 'first come first served' basis. This was issued by the market policeman and had to be worn on the sleeve so that the market inspector could see it. Anyone found hawking without a licence, or not displaying it properly, or borrowing one from someone else, was fined. The town also employed a rat-catcher in the

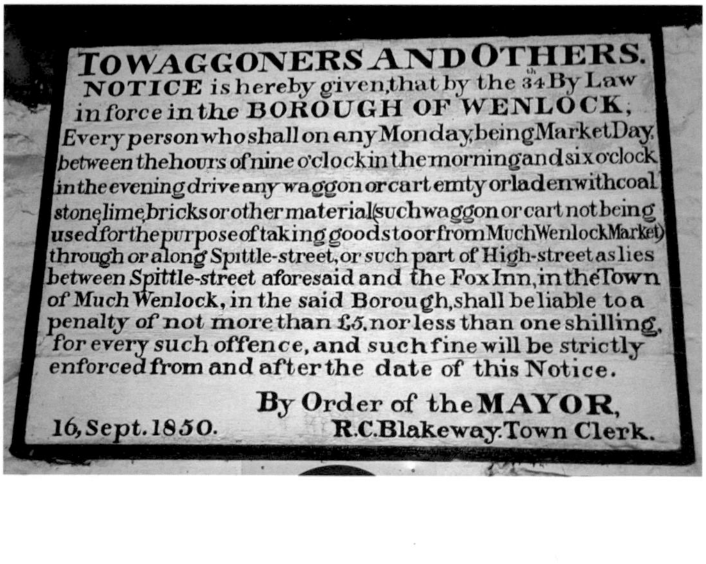

Notice 'TO WAGGONERS AND OTHERS' in the market area under the Guildhall, Much Wenlock (Shropshire).

ABOVE
Market Place, Guildhall and church, Much Wenlock (Shropshire).

Bull Ring market. Rats and other vermin were caught with the help of a ferret and terrier.

To avoid traffic congestion in small market towns, strict rules might have to be imposed. A board attached to the wall in the market area underneath the Guildhall at Much Wenlock (Shropshire) warns 'waggoners and others' not to bring 'any waggon or cart empty or laden with coal, stone, lime, bricks or any other material (such wagon or cart not being used for the purpose of taking goods to or from Much Wenlock Market)' through a certain part of the town. The fine for breaking this rule, dating to 1850, was 'not more than £5 nor less than one shilling'.

WEIGHTS AND MEASURES

Local authorities had a duty to ensure that customers were not deceived in any way, either by being sold inferior goods or by being overcharged or sold short measure. To this end, between the twelfth and nineteenth centuries regular assizes were held – often weekly – to determine the price of such staples as bread and ale, taking into account the cost of a bushel of wheat in the local area. Also weights and measures had to be checked. The document from Helmsley (Yorkshire) mentioned above commands official investigators to 'Inquire of those who have and use false weights and measures and whether the Assize of bread and ale be just'.

To ensure that honesty prevailed, a set of public weights and measures would be kept at the guildhall or town hall so that those used by traders could be measured against them. In addition some regularly used measures might be kept in the parish church. In Ambleside (Cumbria) the pint and quart measures still to be seen in the church of St Mary the Virgin were used to check those used by market traders. In Bromyard (Herefordshire) a metal bushel measure with two handles and standing on four short feet, dating to 1670, is kept in St Peter's Church.

Though weights and measures often varied from one part of the country to another, and even between adjacent regions, from early on the aim was to standardise these nationally. Already in the tenth century, during the reign of Edgar the Peaceful, the rule was that all measures should be the same and that standard sets must be kept in London and Winchester (Hampshire), the two centres of

Stone carving above the door of the Tolbooth and Weigh-house, Ceres (Fife), showing a weigh-beam, bale of cloth, weights and the inscription 'GOD BLESS THE JUST'.

government. Magna Carta, signed by King John in 1215, had a number of clauses reiterating the importance of national standards. One of its rulings states: 'Let there be one measure of wine throughout our Kingdom and one measure of ale and one measure of corn ... let it be the same with weights as with measures.' Yet in 1602 Richard Carew in his *Survey of Cornwall* wrote: 'In measures the shire varieth, not only from others, but also in itself; for they have a land measure and a water measure. The land measure differeth in divers places, from eighteen to twenty-four gallons, the bushel, being least in the eastern parts, and increasing to the westward, where they measure oats by the hogshead. The justices of peace have oftentimes endeavoured to reduce this variance to a certainty...'

Successive monarchs tried to ensure that every part of the country complied with nationally laid-down standards and where new charters were granted this would be emphasised. So the market charter obtained by Roger de Clifford of Kirkby Stephen (Cumbria) in 1353 demanded that traders should 'use lawful weights and measures, upon pain to forfeit the value of their traces and merchandise'. In 1357 it was ordained that sets of balances and standard weights should be sent to all the sheriffs in England. In 1497 Henry VII had new sets of weights sent to thirty-seven county towns and five other important cities or ports, and under Elizabeth I, in 1588, fifty-seven towns and cities received new weights. In 1601 new standards for measures were introduced by the Exchequer. On each occasion the weights and measures were stamped with the coat of arms of the reigning monarch. The accuracy of measures became particularly important for excise reasons when tax was introduced after the Restoration of the monarchy in 1660.

The arrangements for checking the weights and measures used by traders differed from place to place. In Machynlleth (Powys) the coroner had the task of ensuring that the correct yard measure was used. In most towns ale conners tested both the quality of the ale and the measures used in alehouses and taverns, whilst bread weighers checked the quality and weight of loaves. (Amongst other places, Ashburton in Devon and Alcester in Warwickshire still enact the ancient custom of Bread Weighing and Ale Tasting.) In eighteenth-century Morpeth (Northumberland) the order came 'that the Breadweighers shall upon every markett day or when the bread is presented

Set of six weights of Edward III (1327–77) in Winchester City Museum (Hampshire): 91 lb, 56 lb, 28 lb, 14 lb, 7 lb, 7 lb. (By kind permission of Winchester City Council Museums Service, photographer R. M. Pendreigh).

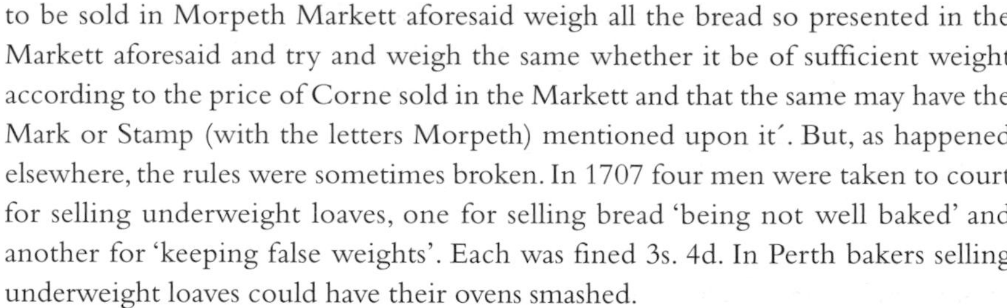

to be sold in Morpeth Markett aforesaid weigh all the bread so presented in the Markett aforesaid and try and weigh the same whether it be of sufficient weight according to the price of Corne sold in the Markett and that the same may have the Mark or Stamp (with the letters Morpeth) mentioned upon it´. But, as happened elsewhere, the rules were sometimes broken. In 1707 four men were taken to court for selling underweight loaves, one for selling bread 'being not well baked' and another for 'keeping false weights'. Each was fined 3s. 4d. In Perth bakers selling underweight loaves could have their ovens smashed.

Towards the end of the eighteenth century men such as James Watt and John Whitehurst were working towards new standard weights to replace the traditional local ones. This was finally achieved by Robert Bettell Bate, mathematical instrument maker to HM Excise, who, following an Act of Parliament of 1825, made models for new standard weights and measures that were used to supply hundreds of sets to government and municipal offices throughout the country. Many local authorities still have full or partial sets of weights and measures, often dating to different periods, on display in town halls or museums. Examples can be found in the Jewel Tower of the former Palace of Westminster, Shugborough Estate County Museum, the Huntley House Museum in Edinburgh, the City Museum in Winchester (Hampshire), Lincoln's Guildhall, the Potteries Museum and Art Gallery, Stoke-on-Trent (Staffordshire), Wycombe Museum at High Wycombe (Buckinghamshire), the Penlee Art Gallery Museum in Penzance (Cornwall) and Stranraer Museum (Dumfries and Galloway). The set shown in the Guildhall of Much Wenlock (Shropshire) was bought in 1853 for £87 3s. 6d.

ABOVE
Set of imperial measures, Shugborough Estate County Museum, near Stafford.

BELOW
The Bell and Steelyard, Woodbridge (Suffolk). Here the steelyard used to weigh wagons before and after market is still in place.

In the second half of the eighteenth century John Wyatt of Birmingham invented an overhead steelyard for the weighing of loaded carts. This became very popular with corporations wanting to stop evasion of market tolls. In Woodbridge (Suffolk) the Bell and Steelyard inn still has the steelyard used to weigh carts before and after market, with the difference in weight indicating the tolls to be paid. Sling chains were passed under a wagon and the steelyard was raised by tackle until the slings became taut. The 108-lb lead poise was then pushed along the steelyard until the leverage lifted the wagon. This was last used in the 1880s. In a former museum in Norfolk Street, King's Lynn (Norfolk) can be found the beam of a similar overhead steelyard, which belonged to the Blue Lion near the now-demolished East Gate.

Many towns had a weigh-house (in Scotland it was called a 'tron), in which the official weigh-beam was kept. Anyone could use this against the payment of a fee. In Bath (Somerset) this amenity was attached to the combined guildhall and market building, with access to it from outside. An interesting example of a weigh-house can be found in Ceres (Fifc); together with the former tolbooth, it is now a museum. An eyecatching carving above the door shows a parcel being weighcd on a set of scales, with the motto 'GOD BLESS THE JUST'. In Uttoxeter (Staffordshire) the Weighing Machine, a classical building dating to 1854, is still standing in the Market Place, where Samuel Johnson once did penance for disobeying his father. In the Grainger Market in Newcastle-upon-Tyne, opened in 1835, the Weigh House is still in use. Some Scottish towns have reminders of their former tron buildings. In Edinburgh Tron Kirk stands close to the site of the former weigh-house and in Glasgow the Tron Steeple in Trongate rises above the building in which the weigh-beam used to be kept. In Dumfries the weigh-house was situated in the Midsteeple or town hall.

ABOVE
The weighing machine house, Uttoxeter (Staffordshire), built in the classical style by Thomas Fradgley in 1854. Within a recess is a panel showing Dr Samuel Johnson doing penance for disobeying his father. (The young Samuel had been asked by his father to attend the latter's bookstall in Uttoxeter when the father was ill, but he refused.) Dr Johnson told a friend how, fifty years to the day after the event, he had 'uncovered [his] head and stood with it bare an hour before the stall which [his] father had formerly used, exposed to the sneers of the standers-by and in the inclemency of the weather…'

For the measurement of fabric, ell-sticks or yardsticks were employed. Traditionally the English ell (from the Latin *ulna*, arm) was based on the length of the arm of Henry I. Though a quick way to measure this length would be by extending the material between the end of one's nose and the fingertips of an outstretched arm, official yardsticks ensured that there could be no cheating. An ell should measure 45 inches and an inch three barleycorns. Four inches was a palm and 9 inches a span. The City Museum in Winchester has a bronze hexagonal stick, dating from the reign of Henry VII, which has a terminal showing the letter H at one end and the letter E at the other to indicate that the bar was adjusted in the reign of Queen Elizabeth I. Official measures were often fastened to public buildings so that people could check for fraud. In Dunkeld (Perth and Kinross) a metal stick measuring an ell is attached to the 'Ell Shop' in the marketplace. As a reminder of the former importance of this public amenity, a nineteenth-century plaque on the late twentieth-century market building in Lancaster lists the imperial standard measures, 'AT 62 FAHRENHEIT VERIFIED BY THE STANDARD DEPARTMENT BOARD OF TRADE 1879'.

LEFT
The Weigh House, Grainger Market, Newcastle-upon-Tyne.

The Dunkeld Ell, attached to a building in the Market Place, Dunkeld (Perth and Kinross).

Though the checking of weights and measures continues as trading standards are upheld, this is no longer done in public. However, remembering the past, the mayor of Barnstaple (Devon) each year, at the beginning of the End of Harvest Fair, re-enacts the testing of the official scales, which used to be done to ensure honest trading in the Pannier Market.

CRIME AND PUNISHMENT

Magna Carta states: 'A free man shall not be amerced [that is fined – the offender is said to be "in mercy" and the money paid to settle the matter was called "amercement"] for a trivial offence, except in accordance with the degree of the offence, and for a serious offence he shall be amerced according to its gravity.'

Markets provide opportunities for dishonest behaviour, by both traders and visitors. Those attending might make nuisances of themselves by stealing or committing assault. Those breaking the law had to be punished, sometimes by a fine, sometimes by physical chastisement. Cases would be tried in the local court, often situated in the guildhall, town hall or moot hall, or the Scottish tolbooth, where usually the cells could be found. Often special constables were appointed, who would check on market proceedings. In livestock markets it could be difficult to keep an eye on every animal for sale and theft sometimes occurred. In sixteenth-century Glamis (Angus) Rory Mclean had twenty-four 'fat ky' stolen in the market. In the same period Henry Chamber of Hingham (Norfolk) was sent to jail for 'drawing off the pursse of Henry Coleman of Wymondham lynnen wever' in Wymondham (Norfolk) market. In 1291 in Great Yarmouth (Norfolk) Walter de Clippesby was accused of assault after he had seized a jug of milk from Felicia Nigrum in the marketplace and broken it over her head.

As has already been mentioned, stallholders could cheat in a number of ways, from giving short measure to offering inferior goods for sale, or by breaking the rules

The 'cage' or lock-up for offenders underneath the guildhall and market hall of Titchfield (Hampshire), now in the Weald and Downland Open Air Museum at Singleton (Sussex).

against middlemen. Sometimes a list of set fines assisted the courts dealing with these matters. In 1523 in Morpeth (Northumberland) the lord of the manor, Lord Dacre, issued a set of regulations covering the various trades carried out in the town within the seven guilds. Set fines were imposed where general, often universal rules were broken. As happened in other towns, only approved traders, that is members of the Merchant Guild, were allowed to sell their goods. (In 1261 Windsor dealers attacked merchants from Reading, trampling their goods in the mud.) Anyone breaking this rule would be fined 6s. 8d. Merchants found to have been trading before the starting bell or who were found 'cheapening' (negotiating) before they 'present[ed] to market' could face a payment of the same amount (half to be paid to the lord). Members of the Weavers' Guild paid 2s. 10d if it was found that they had mixed hair or flock with their wool. Anyone found buying goods in the market and reselling them close by was fined 40d.

The court roll covering the years 1390–1 for Great Yarmouth (Norfolk) reveals that Alice Goodgroom and John Lokard were prosecuted for hoarding eggs in order to raise their price in the market. In 1546 in Burford (Oxfordshire) Simon Wisdom, Richard Hedges, Edmund Sylvester and Robert Burton were amerced 6d each for making excessive profits from fish, and in 1547 Wisdom was amerced again, for a larger sum, though no charge was recorded. In Barnstaple (Devon) it was noted in the town's records that in 1612 the sum of 3d was paid for 'watching flesh hung up on the [High] Cross in Lent'. As eating meat during Lent was against the rules, this must have served as a warning as well as a punishment.

The stocks and market in Moreton-in-Marsh (Gloucestershire).

Sometimes offenders were condemned to a spell in the stocks or pillory, two instruments of punishment that could usually be found in the marketplace. In England the 1351 Statute of Labourers required every town to provide a set of stocks so that people committing relatively minor crimes could be punished in full view of the community – often on market days for greater effectiveness. In Scotland an Act of Parliament of 1574 stated that local officials were to provide and repair irons and stocks for the punishment of wrongdoers, including those convicted of being drunk, begging or swearing. An English statute of 1495 said that vagabonds should be set in the stocks with only bread and water as nourishment. On release the prisoner often felt numb and was scarcely able to walk away.

The pillory was used for more serious offences. This was a much harsher punishment as it could lead to death. Not being able to defend themselves against attacks from the public, as the

In the stocks. *A passer-by is mocking the miscreants. (From the M.S. 10E. IV.)*

head and hands were immobilised, those punished were sometimes left permanently maimed or blinded. The pillory might also serve as a whipping post, used for birching or caning, and sometimes for branding or the removal of an ear. In Glasgow the custom of lug-pinning (nailing the ear of a criminal to the Tolbooth door) was eventually discontinued as it 'corrupted community life, weavers will leave their looms and children play truant' in order to make fun of the miscreant. Here also metal rings in the walls of the Tolbooth steeple were used for chaining people up as a punishment. Some market crosses doubled as whipping posts, having cuffs attached, to which hands were fastened. This can be observed in Bungay (Suffolk), whilst in Much Wenlock (Shropshire) and New Buckenham (Norfolk) arm clamps are incorporated in the market buildings. As late as 1799, local officials in Ludlow were admonished for failing to provide a new whipping post. In Milnthorpe (Cumbria) the eighteenth-century market cross with its ball finial has iron ankle cuffs welded into the steps of the base. In Scotland an iron neck ring, or jougs, often attached to the market cross or tolbooth, could be used to immobilise an offender. This was done in Crail (Fife) and in Crieff

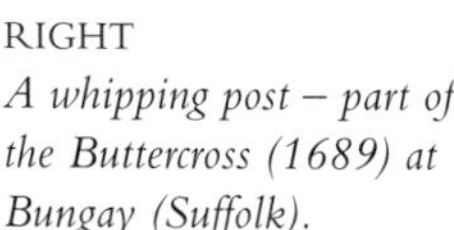

RIGHT
A whipping post – part of the Buttercross (1689) at Bungay (Suffolk).

FAR RIGHT
Jougs, a metal neck collar, now attached to the west end of Monzie church (Perth and Kinross), was formerly used to chain up an offender.

Mobile stocks at Much Wenlock Guildhall (Shropshire).

(Perth and Kinross), where the ninth-century market cross, now kept in the cells of the former town hall, still has the remains of the jougs attached to it. Examples can be seen hanging by the main door of the Tolbooth and Weigh House in Ceres (Fife), and attached to Kilmaurs Town House (Ayrshire) and to the west end of the parish church of Monzie (Perth and Kinross). Kirkcudbright Tolbooth (Dumfries and Galloway) has two sets of jougs, and in Fochabers (Moray) a Tuscan column, formerly used as the market cross, retains the chain of some jougs. Occasionally a criminal's hair was cut off as further humiliation.

Though in England the pillory was abolished in 1837, the stocks never were and many can still be found in or near market areas, for instance in Stow-on-the-Wold, Moreton-in-Marsh and Winchcombe (all in Gloucestershire) and (a replica) in Woodstock (Oxfordshire). Some are kept in museums and other places of interest. The stocks kept in the former town hall of Crieff (Perth and Kinross) are unique in that they are made of metal and could accommodate four people at once. The Guildhall (above the market building) of Much Wenlock (Shropshire) contains a mobile set of stocks, with room for three miscreants, which could be pushed about on wheels. In Wimborne Minster (Dorset) the White Hart in the Cornmarket has the handcuffs that were used on offenders awaiting their turn in the stocks. There are few pillories left but one of these is stored in the attic of the town hall in Rye (Sussex). The last recorded use of stocks occurred in 1873 in Newbury (Berkshire).

THE PAYMENT OF TOLLS

As mentioned earlier, markets not only facilitated the trading of goods but also provided an income for those who held the rights to them: the lord of the manor, a religious institution which may have had the proceeds assigned to it, or the citizens of a town (who might have been able to buy this privilege after the dissolution of the monasteries at the time of Henry VIII). In Canterbury Henry II, walking barefoot through the marketplace on his way to the cathedral as penance for the murder of Thomas Becket in 1170, allocated 'forever' the royal market tolls to the leper hospital in Harbledown (Kent), amounting to ten silver marks. Now an almshouse, the charity still receives an annual cheque for £13.33.

In Saxon times a merchant usually paid either a daily charge or an amount that was proportional to the profits he had made. Later the income came from tolls (tollage), rent paid for stalls (stallage) and fines imposed for the breaking of market rules. Traders were charged for every animal and every cartload of goods offered for sale. In Domesday Book it is stated that in Lewes (Sussex) 'whoever sells a horse in the burgh gives a coin to the reeve, and he who buys, another. For an ox, a half-penny. For a man 4 pence.' In Lichfield (Staffordshire) the list of goods on which tolls should be paid in 1299 included horses, cattle, pigs, sheep, fresh salmon, eels, herring, conger, salted and fresh meat, honey, garlic, oil, wine and fleeces. At that time the lord of the manor, Bishop Roger de Clinton, received approximately £6 per year in tolls. In Burford (Oxfordshire) tolls amounted to a quadrans (a farthing) for a thousand nails or a hundred horseshoes, an obo (half a penny) for each horse, ox or cow, or hide of them, and a denarius (silver penny) for a silk cloth embroidered with gold. In 1337 the market tolls were worth 50s. In sixteenth-century Machynlleth (Powys) all those engaged in the sale of grain, salt, apples and seeds in the street paid a proportion of their goods to the Sergeant-at-Mace. The authorities also charged each buyer and seller coming into the town a toll of a penny, to be put towards the income of the borough. Toll stones (now in the Owain Glyndwr Institute) were put at three strategic points, ensuring that all traders had to pass one on their way to market.

BELOW
List of tolls on one of the toll stones that were originally placed at Pentrerhedyn Street, Doll Street and on Parliament House in Maengwyn Street, Machynlleth (Powys). The stones are now kept in the Owain Glyndwr Institute in Maengwyn Street.

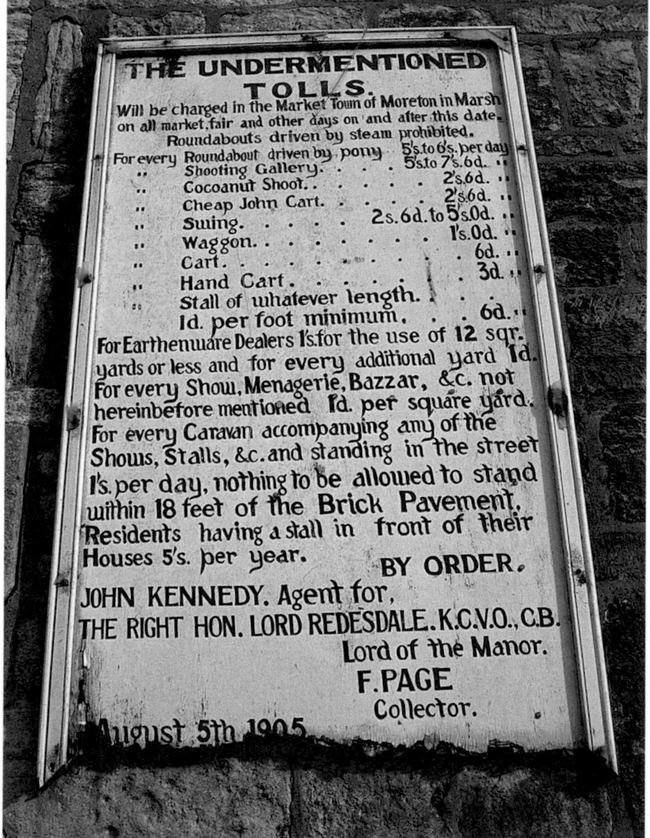

BELOW RIGHT
List of tolls on the Curfew Tower in Moreton-in-Marsh (Gloucestershire).

Probably dating to the eighteenth century, they list the various dues to be paid. In the early nineteenth-century market building in Dartmouth (Devon), boards list the tolls that were charged, including the following: 'For every Basket, Parcel or quantity of Butter exceeding six and not exceeding twelve pounds, two pence and for every additional quantity not exceeding six pounds, one penny. Fowls, Chickens, Ducks, Wildfowls or Rabbits one half penny each. For every Turkey, Goose or Sucking Pig One Penny. Pigeons One Penny Pr Basket. Eggs, one half Penny per Dozen. Potatoes, One Penny pr Bag. For every Pannier, Basket, Firkin, Barrel, Tub or Mound of Fruit, One Penny. Cockles, Muscles, Wrinkles One Half Penny pr Basket or Parcel. Lobsters, Crabs, Oysters, One Penny per Basket, Hamper or Parcel.' The lists of tolls attached to the exterior of the Curfew Tower overlooking the marketplace of

The Curfew Tower, Moreton-in-Marsh (Gloucestershire).

RIGHT
The tolzey at Burford (Oxfordshire).

BELOW
The tolzey and two conduits in front of All Saints' Church, Bristol. In the open arcaded area merchants would conduct their business. In the mid eighteenth century the Exchange built nearby to the design of John Wood the Elder of Bath took over its role.

Moreton-in-Marsh and in the Market House of Tetbury (both in Gloucestershire) are also very comprehensive. The lord of the manor of Halstead (Essex) still receives the stallholders' tolls for the Saturday market.

Often the tolls would be collected at the entrance into a town or marketplace, in the tolbooth or tolzey or in the market house. In Modbury (Devon) the Chain House in Brownston Street is believed to have been the tollhouse, where on market days chains were stretched across the road which would be lowered only when toll had been paid. Tetbury had two tolzeys: one opposite the Market House and one on the corner of The Chipping and Chipping Street. A nineteenth-century drawing of All Saints' Church, Bristol, shows the tolzey and two conduits attached to the church, which also has a covered market area in front of it. Burford (Oxfordshire), Ludlow (Shropshire) and Wotton-under-Edge (Gloucestershire) still have former tolzeys. The building in Burford (now a museum) was erected by the Guild of Merchants in the sixteenth century and continues to have an open ground floor, providing shelter for stalls. In Ludlow and Wotton-under-Edge the structures are now used as shops. In Norwich the remains of the former tollhouse can be seen in the fourteenth-century undercroft of the Guildhall.

In Morpeth a toll collector stood at the north end of the bridge across the River Wansbeck, charging traders as they came in. According to the Reverend John Hodgson, writing in 1832, the tolls were as follows: 'every horned beast coming into this market for sale 1d; every pig and calf, 1/2d; and the widows of poor freemen pay a dishful of corn for every poke [bag] set upon the pavement for sale…' In a number of towns street names remind of the former presence of tolzeys. In Beverley (Yorkshire) people wanting to trade paid their dues at a cross standing on the corner of Cross Street and Toll Gavel ('gavel' means 'rent'). In Tewkesbury (Gloucestershire) Tolsey Lane comes off the High Street, close to the town hall.

In Scotland a burgh's tolbooth often combined the functions of town hall, court, jail for criminals and debtors, indoor market, weigh-house and toll collection point, with a central administrative body in charge. For this reason they are usually prominent buildings. This is not unlike the situation that developed in England, where the town hall might have incorporated an open market, a courtroom and cells and also have acted as the repository of the official weights and measures. Former tolbooth buildings can be found in many Scottish towns and cities, amongst them Edinburgh, where it is used as a museum; Glasgow, with only the steeple left, where prisoners were kept on the top floor, as was also the case in Falkirk's town steeple, now without the tolbooth that once adjoined it. As was also the case in Falkirk's town steeple, now without the tolbooth that once adjoined it; the Crail (Fife) where the ground floor is used as a library; Lauder (Scottish Borders); Dysart (Fife); Dalkeith (Midlothian); Tain (Highland); and the example at Kirkcudbright (Dumfries and Galloway), now an arts centre. The tolbooth in Sanquhar (Dumfries and Galloway), now converted into a museum, was built by William Adam, brother of the celebrated architect Robert Adam, and is the only building of its type designed by him.

It must not be forgotten that today's market traders, too, pay rent, either to the local authorities or to a private organisation.

Tolbooth, Canongate, Edinburgh (1591). Here tolls were collected. The building also served as a town hall, courtroom and prison for the Canongate. The clock, dating from 1820, replaces a seventeenth-century predecessor. It now houses 'The People's Story'.

H.J. and D.E. Hicks and Son.
Newsagent
Alfriston Antique
The Singing Kettle

Chapter Three

MARKET CROSSES AND MARKET BUILDINGS

'THER is in the marketplace of the toun a new cross of six arches, and a piller yn the middle for market folks to stande yn, begon and brought up to fornix by Ely laste abate of Brutun...' wrote John Leland in his description of Bruton, Somerset, in 1542.

When in the thirteenth century markets were banned from churches and churchyards, traders moved their stalls to other prominent areas in town, often in front of or near to the church. In these new marketplaces it was common for dealers to gather around a newly erected market cross. This representative of the hallowed ground left behind was a reminder that business should be conducted honestly, 'in the sight of God'. (In the early nineteenth century Bishop John Milner wrote: 'the general intent of market crosses was to inspire public homage to the religion of Christ crucified and to inspire men with a sense of morality and piety amongst the ordinary transactions in life'.)

The market cross stood at the centre of what in a later age would be described as the 'central business district', marking the area where the prosperity of the community was, to a large extent, generated. In addition it acted as a general focal point for local society as here important announcements would be made, contracts sealed, bargains struck, disputes settled, tolls collected and punishments meted out. Here also preachers, from medieval friars to John Wesley (1703–91), spoke to the crowds on religious matters. Sometimes it was at the centre of political affairs, as at Newport (Cornwall), now part of Launceston, where in 1829 a small building was erected over the shaft of an ancient cross, to create what became known as 'Newport Town Hall'. In this place members of Parliament for this separate borough were proposed and seconded. In Carlisle (Cumbria) the Market or Carel Cross is topped by a lion resting a paw on a representation of the Dormont Book, an ancient document, part of which survives in the town hall, containing important by-laws of the city. In Scotland the mercat cross was the symbol of burgh status and the right of a town's citizens to trade. Here a law passed by King William I (1165–1214) required that all goods for sale be presented at a central mercat cross, of which around 126 still survive.

Amongst the many proclamations issued from market crosses in different parts of Britain is the one commemorated by a plaque on the remains of the cross by St Leonard's Tower in Newton Abbot (Devon), which states that here 'THE FIRST DECLARATION OF WILLIAM, PRINCE OF ORANGE [the future William III], THE GLORIOUS DEFENDER OF THE PROTESTANT RELIGION AND THE LIBERTIES OF ENGLAND, WAS READ ON THIS PEDESTAL BY

OPPOSITE
The market cross in Alfriston (Sussex). Its head has been lost.

BELOW
Carel Cross, Carlisle (Cumbria), 1682. A lion rests a paw on a representation of the Dormont Book, an ancient document (part of which survives in the town hall) containing important by-laws of the city. Note the sundial.

THE REV. JOHN REYNEL RECTOR OF THIS PARISH, ON 5th NOVEMBER 1688'. In 1715 Lord Derwentwater, arriving with 370 horsemen in Morpeth (Northumberland), where he hoped to find more followers, proclaimed James, son of the exiled James II, king in the marketplace. On a less exalted level, the opening of the all-important charter fairs, which took place in many towns at different times of the year, was often announced from the steps of the market cross. In Melton Mowbray (Leicestershire) the Butter or High Cross played an unusual role in the period after the Civil War as a place where marriage banns were read on three successive Tuesdays, followed by a wedding in the Market Place. In this way 158 couples made their vows in front of the local magistrates. Even in the nineteenth century the local authorities of Wigtown (Dumfries and Galloway) stipulated that the site where the old and new crosses had been brought together should be the location from where 'all proclamations, publications and intimations shall be made'.

In seventeenth-century Scotland Charles I decreed that all public executions should take place at the mercat cross (which often incorporates a depiction of a unicorn, the heraldic supporter for the Scottish royal arms). In England and Wales, too, criminals were dealt with in this public place, as were heretics condemned to be burned at the stake. In addition, this was the site where the heads or other body parts of rebels would be displayed as a deterrent, and to convince citizens of the death of someone who, when alive, might have attracted followers for renewed attacks. After the battle of Shrewsbury, on 21 July 1403, the body of Henry Percy (Harry Hotspur) was left by Shrewsbury's market cross before parts of it were distributed around the country.

In Edinburgh the Mercat Cross has had five different sites since 1365. The present cross, situated close to St Giles' Cathedral, dates from 1885 and incorporates remains of a fifteenth-century predecessor in the shaft. Nearby an outline of the second cross, in situ *till 1756, can be found in the cobbles.*

The view of the market cross as the geographical centre of a community is further demonstrated by the fact that all distances between towns were measured from the market cross. When Penzance (Cornwall) was incorporated on 9 May 1614 the boundary was drawn half a mile from the market cross. The 13-foot-long shaft of the late thirteenth-century market cross at Irthlingborough (Northamptonshire) was useful in another way – as the standard for the 'pole', an agricultural measurement used in the medieval field system. In Leicestershire the territories of the Belvoir, Quorn and Cottesmore hunts adjoin at the marketplace of Melton Mowbray.

As will be seen, structures described as a 'market cross' are not necessarily in the shape of a crucifix and may not include even a reference to this Christian symbol. They come shaped as pillars, slender turrets, obelisks, cones and shelters in a wide range of sizes and designs. The first market crosses may have been based on early crosses found in the churchyards that had been vacated by traders, such as the carved Saxon shafts at Wolverhampton (14 feet high) and Masham (Yorkshire), both dating to the ninth century, and Stapleford (Nottinghamshire), with its early eleventh-century decoration. Other examples include the medieval crosses at Bishop's Lydeard (Somerset) and Tyberton (Herefordshire) – the former topped with a cross, the latter with a carving of the Virgin Mary and Child on one side and a crucifix on the other – and

FAR LEFT
The Anglo-Saxon cross in St Peter's churchyard, Wolverhampton.

LEFT
Medieval market cross in Downpatrick (Down, Northern Ireland).

Highley (Shropshire), which has lost its head. All stand on steps. The Mercat Cross of Melrose (Scottish Borders) originally stood in the abbey precinct.

The small, extensively carved market cross of Downpatrick (Down) has a Celtic wheel-head, as has the more basic eleventh-century granite cross formerly standing in the Green Market of Penzance (Cornwall). However, most early market crosses, much copied in later centuries, consist of a shaft inserted in a socket, which may or may not stand on steps. Generally the upper end of the shaft ends in a ring, the knop, above which rises the head, sometimes in the shape of a lantern, perhaps decoratively carved with biblical illustrations, and sometimes featuring a cross. Some market crosses are lifted up high, on top of a number of steps. This can be seen in Lambourn (Berkshire), Repton and Bonsall (both in Derbyshire), Winsford (Cheshire), Alnwick (Northumberland), Doune (Stirling) – though here originally the cross stood on just one step – Cheadle (Staffordshire) and Lydney (Gloucestershire). In Lavenham (Suffolk) a substantial height is achieved via the three very steep steps on which the market cross (probably a former churchyard cross) rests, whilst in Alfriston (Sussex) the socket of the simple shaft with knop (the head has been lost) has been placed high up on a brick-built base situated on an island in the former market area. The pillar with ball finial given by Dame Dorothy Brown in 1727 (so reads the inscription on this newly restored monument) stands on four substantial steps in the marketplace at Darlington (Durham). In 1697, during her 'Northern Journey', Celia Fiennes travelled through Doncaster (Yorkshire), where she saw 'a handsome Market Cross advanc'ed on 20 steps at least…'

BELOW
Medieval cross in St Mary's churchyard, Tyberton (Herefordshire). It has a crucifix on one side and a seated Virgin with Child under a canopy on the other.

Only part of the medieval shaft is now left, moved from its original site in 1793. Less elevated examples are found in Stow-on-the-Wold (Gloucestershire), Milnthorpe (Cumbria), and Chester. The fifteenth-century Butter Cross in Winchester (Hampshire), tucked away in a corner where the High Street briefly widens out, is in the shape of a delicate spire on steps.

On market days the stone steps of a cross could be very useful for the display of produce. Even today traders sometimes provide a colourful sight as they show their wares in this way. The splendid market cross built in 1814 in Devizes (Wiltshire) has an interesting inscription relating the cautionary tale of one Ruth Pierce of Potterne 'in this county', who on 25 January 1753 agreed with three other women

> to buy a sack of wheat in the market each paying her due proportion towards the same. One of these women in collecting these several quotas of money discovered a deficiency and demanded of Ruth Pierce the same which was wanting to make good the amount. Ruth Pierce protested that she had paid her share and said she wished she might drop down dead if she had not. She rashly repeated this awful wish when to the consternation and terror of the surrounding multitude she instantly fell down and expired having the money concealed in her hand.

Curiously, the market cross at Over (Cheshire) incorporates in its huge stepped base a former lock-up supporting a small plain cross. In Deeping St James (Lincolnshire) the fifteenth-century cross lost its shaft when in 1819 the base was converted into a cell for up to three people, who would be kept there overnight before being taken in front of the magistrates the next morning. It is said that sometimes prisoners were served tea from a long-spouted kettle thrust through the bars of the oak door, through which three seats and wall-mounted manacles can still be seen.

BELOW LEFT
Medieval market cross in Lambourn (Berkshire). Note the similarity with the cross in Tyberton churchyard (Herefordshire), shown on page 53.

BELOW RIGHT
The fifteenth-century market cross at Deeping St James (Lincolnshire) was turned into a lock-up in 1819 after its shaft had been taken down.

Where markets thrived and communities prospered, some of the surplus money becoming available might be spent on an enlarged and enhanced market cross, as an expression of civic pride, but also to provide shelter for traders and their produce, and for toll collectors and other officials. In some places this meant a roofed structure, open at ground level, being added around the original cross. Leland gives an interesting description of this development in Lichfield (Staffordshire), where, he writes: 'There used to be a fine old cross with steps around it in [the] Market Place. But Dean Denton has recently spent £160 in enclosing the cross within a structure of 8 fine arches, surmounted by a round vault, to enable poor market traders to stand in the dry.' A further description mentions that attached to it were 'two crucifixes, about xviii or xx inches in length, very artificially cast in brass; on the top of the carved railes and banisters, being bound through with iron rods, was placed viii of our Saviour's Apostles, about iv foot in height, each carrying the emblem of their death, curiously carved to the life, in their several habets, and below them was cut in the stone the founder's coat of armes.' This no longer exists as it was 'utterly destroyed [in the Civil War] because a cross', but similar structures do survive.

The former market cross in Lichfield (Staffordshire), enhanced in the early sixteenth century by Dean Denton, who enclosed the original structure with roofed arches, surmounted by eight statues and two brass crucifixes. Note the bell and stocks.

In Castle Combe (Wiltshire) and Cheddar (Somerset) the medieval cross is enclosed in this way, with the top of the shaft and head left to rise above the roof. This is not the case in Somerton (Somerset), where in 1673 the whole cross was covered by a roof shaped like a pyramid. In Shepton Mallet (Somerset) the tall pinnacle, donated, together with an endowment to maintain it, by Agnes and Walter Buckland in 1500 (as stated on the original plaque inside), is very visible above the later shelter, possibly added in 1700. (As a further amenity a plate listing the distances to various towns, starting with London, is attached to it.) In Bingley (Yorkshire) not only is the medieval cross surrounded by a square structure, with the head of the cross appearing above its roof, but a further enlargement was provided in 1753, when a market house of five bays was attached to it. The stone pillar of the Butter Cross in Oakham (Rutland), already depicted on Speed's map of 1611, sticks out above the large wooden roof providing shelter. In Pembridge (Herefordshire) the remains of a

FAR LEFT
In Cheddar (Somerset) the fifteenth-century cross was enclosed, possibly in the seventeenth century, by an embattled shelter. Here the top of the shaft and head rise above the roof.

LEFT
A sign on the sixteenth-century market cross (with later shelter) in Shepton Mallet (Somerset) informs travellers of the distances to London and various West Country towns.

In Oakham (Rutland) the stone pillar of the Butter Cross sticks out above the large polygonal roof sheltering the stocks. It probably dates to the seventeenth century.

medieval cross can be seen at the base of one of the eight carved posts carrying the roof. The steeply pitched, gabled canopy (surmounted by a clock turret with cupola) of the seventeenth-century Butter Cross in Witney (Oxfordshire) shelters an older pillar mounted on stone steps.

In a number of towns quite elaborate market shelters were erected and, though many of these have been lost – the cross in Bruton (Somerset) and Dean Denton's market cross in Lichfield (Staffordshire) amongst them – there are still some interesting examples enhancing the urban landscape. One of the most striking of these is the highly decorated cross in Chichester (Sussex), built in 1501 by Bishop Story as a focal point for the former marketplace. It has a lantern at the top, a clock and a bronze bust of Charles I, added after the Restoration. Other, similarly arched stone-built structures can be found in Malmesbury (Wiltshire) – in the sixteenth

The Market Hall in Pembridge (Herefordshire) in 1842. On the right is the seventeenth-century New Inn, which had a courtroom on the first floor and a cell, still with its window bars, on the lower level.

FAR LEFT
The Market Cross in Chichester (Sussex) was built in 1501 by Bishop Story. It has a lantern at the top, a clock, and a bronze bust of Charles I, added after the Restoration.

LEFT
The cross at Malmesbury (Wiltshire) was described in the sixteenth century by John Leland as 'a right faire costly peace of worke'.

century described by Leland as 'a right faire costly peace of worke' – and Salisbury (Wiltshire). In Dunster (Somerset) stands the much-photographed octagonal Yarn Market, and in Mildenhall (Suffolk) is a hexagonal shelter with a heavy, low-reaching, intricately constructed wooden roof.

In the eighteenth century newly built or rebuilt market crosses sometimes came in the form of a cupola supported by pillars. Examples can be found in Beverley (Yorkshire), Swaffham (Norfolk) and Mountsorrel (Leicestershire), where the local landowner, Sir John Danvers, built the Buttermarket as a replacement for the old market cross, which he installed in his grounds at Swithland Park. In Bungay (Suffolk) the dome is surmounted by a figure of Justice, complete with sword and scales (unusually, without a blindfold) as a reminder that in the past the Butter Cross was also used as a prison, with a dungeon underneath. One of the pillars doubled up as a

The roof structure of the hexagonal sixteenth-century market cross in Mildenhall (Suffolk).

RIGHT
The Market Cross at Beverley (Yorkshire) was erected in 1711–14. It bears the arms of Queen Anne, the borough and those of the two MPs (Sir Charles Hotham and Sir Michael Warton) who helped pay for it. The cupola is surmounted by a glazed lantern, an obelisk and a weathervane. The vases were added in 1797.

FAR RIGHT
The Butter Cross in Bungay (Suffolk) was built in 1689 and commemorates the great fire of 1688. Note the whipping post.

whipping post as it still has wrist cuffs (at two levels) attached to it. In early eighteenth-century King's Lynn the market cross dating to 1601 (used as a gunpowder store during the Civil War) was no longer deemed worthy of the town and in 1707 the corporation ordered 'the psent decayed cross and the old shambles [to be] taken down' so that it could be replaced by what came to be regarded as one of the 'handsomest market crosses in the country, a masterpiece of Classical Renaissance architecture'. It was flanked by new butchers' shambles and a fish shambles. Built on top of a large well, it eventually started to crack and lean alarmingly so that it had to be demolished in the nineteenth century. A very late market cross is the crenellated octagonal shelter found in the market place of Kirkby Lonsdale (Cumbria). This was presented to the town by the local vicar, the Reverend John Llewelyn Davies, in 1905, on the day before his seventy-ninth birthday.

In contrast to the above-mentioned umbrella-shaped buildings are the rectangular and square market halls, equally made up of a roof carried by arches, as found in Whittlesey (Cambridgeshire), Ilminster (Somerset), Market Drayton (Shropshire), Chippenham (Wiltshire) – all enhanced with Tuscan columns – and Otley (Yorkshire). In Pembridge (Herefordshire) the carved wooden pillars holding up the

The splendid early eighteenth-century market cross, flanked by butchers' and fishmongers' shambles, in King's Lynn (Norfolk). It was pulled down in the nineteenth century after it had become a dangerous structure. (By kind permission of King's Lynn Museum Service)

The stone-built Market Hall in Chipping Campden (Gloucestershire) was erected in 1627 by Sir Baptist Hicks, whose coat of arms can be found on the building.

roof of the early sixteenth-century market hall have notches for the insertion of the boards from which goods would have been sold. The stone-built market hall in Chipping Campden (Gloucestershire) incorporates the coat of arms of the donor, Sir Baptist Hicks, and the date of its construction, 1627. Though not described as a butter cross, it was specifically built for purveyors of dairy produce, providing a cool atmosphere with its stone floor and sheltering roof.

'Butter Cross' is a name which initially may have been applied strictly to the meeting places of those selling dairy produce but then at a later date seems to have come into use as a description of market crosses generally. The reason for this may be the prominent position taken up in the marketplace by those – often farmers' wives – who regularly (without refrigeration, perishable produce could not be kept for long) brought the community the basic foodstuffs it needed. A cross marking this site might reasonably have been referred to as the 'butter cross', with the named commodity representing dairy produce (often including poultry) in general. In this context it is interesting to note that amongst the four crosses in Melton Mowbray (Leicestershire) the Butter Cross was regarded as the High Cross (in places where there was more than one cross, the most important was regarded as the High Cross).

The seventeenth-century Butter Cross in Abbots Bromley (Staffordshire).

A number of butter crosses are without shelter, as is the case at Ireby (Cumbria) and Winchester (Hampshire). The thirteenth-century shaft on steps inside the eighteenth-century market building in Bingley (Yorkshire) was also known by this name before it was enclosed. Other examples offered protection from inclement weather and a cool atmosphere in summer, including those in Abbots Bromley (Staffordshire), Mountsorrel (Leicestershire), Keld (Cumbria) and the already mentioned crosses at Witney (Oxfordshire), Whittlesey (Cambridgeshire),

Chippenham (Wiltshire) and Bungay (Suffolk). A curious example is the butter cross situated near crossroads just outside Alveley (Shropshire). This has a solid circular head with incised Maltese crosses. It has been suggested that this may formerly have been the centre of an open-air market. Very differently shaped is the conical Butter Cross in Hallaton (Leicestershire). This has two ledges on the lower level, which may have been used by country wives to rest their produce-filled baskets on. (This structure plays an important part on Easter Mondays when the annual Hare Pie Scrambling and Bottle Kicking event takes place.) In Melton Mowbray (Leicestershire) the reconstructed Butter Cross stands on the site where during the annual Cheese Fairs pyramids of Stilton cheese were displayed on straw laid out on the cobblestones.

The twentieth-century Buttermarket shopping centre in Ipswich (Suffolk) recalls the elaborate structure observed by Celia Fiennes in 1698, who described it as 'a good Market Cross railed in, I was there on Satturday which is their market day and saw they sold their butter by the pinte, 20 ounces for 6 pence, and often for 5d or 4d. They make it up in a mold just in the shape of a pinte pot and so sell it; their Market Cross has good carving, the figure of Justice carv'd and gilt…'

In addition to butter crosses, buildings known as butter markets exist in a number of places. One of these can be found in Lincoln, built in the classical style in 1737. Another example is the nineteenth-century structure by that name (described in

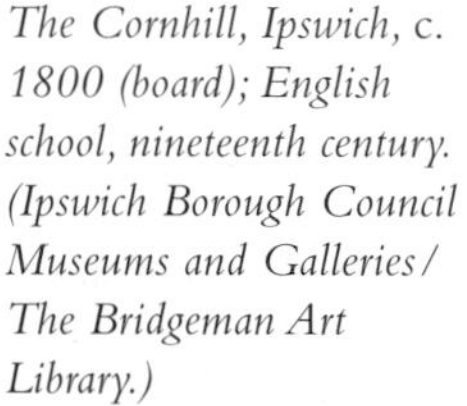

The Cornhill, Ipswich, c. 1800 (board); English school, nineteenth century. (Ipswich Borough Council Museums and Galleries / The Bridgeman Art Library.)

the Pevsner Architectural Guide as 'an uncouth Doric temple') in Market Street, Hay-on-Wye (Powys), where also the Cheese Market of similar date can be found. The much grander classical structure in Ludlow (Shropshire) was built as a council chamber with market space below in 1743–4 and is still used for its original purposes. On market days traders display their goods inside and on the steps leading into the road, adding a colourful aspect to the street scene. The combination of council chamber or town hall above with a butter market below (though in Ludlow the sale of dairy produce does not seem to have been specifically mentioned) is an arrangement that can also be found in Tamworth (Staffordshire), Malton (Yorkshire), Ross-on-Wye (Herefordshire) and Evesham (Worcestershire) – where the butter and poultry market was kept in the undercroft. In Market Harborough (Leicestershire) the butter market was situated underneath the former grammar school, built in 1614. This arrangement was made 'to keepe the market people drye in time of fowle weather'.

ABOVE LEFT
The Market Hall in Ross-on-Wye (Herefordshire) was built of red sandstone between 1660 and 1674. The exterior has a medallion of Charles II.

ABOVE
In Market Harborough (Leicestershire) the area underneath the old grammar school, built in 1614, was used for the weekly butter market.

Some towns had a number of crosses, each associated with a different trade. In Melton Mowbray (Leicestershire) four of the five market areas had a cross, including the Butter Cross (which, as we have seen, probably served as a High Cross), the Sheep Cross, the Corn Cross and the Sage Cross, where vegetables and herbs were sold. All of these were taken down at one time or another. However, towards the end of the twentieth century the Butter Cross and the Corn Cross were recreated, the former with stones belonging to the erstwhile cross found in the churchyard of St Mary's parish church. Alnwick (Northumberland) had eight crosses and Salisbury (Wiltshire) four – the Wool Cross, the Cheese Cross, the Barnewell Cross and, the only one to survive, the Poultry Cross.

In any appreciation of existing market crosses it has to be remembered that the original structure may well have been altered or renewed since it was first built. Many have been moved from their original sites, often to accommodate the needs of traffic, and in the process may have lost one or more features. In 1684 the town council of Forfar (Angus) decided to have a new market cross made by Alexander Adam (believed to be an uncle or great-uncle of the architect William Adam), who obtained stone from Glamis (Angus) in order to do so. Unfortunately he carved some of the heraldic devices required around the tower incorrectly and was told to put this right. Made up of a tower and pillar, it was eventually regarded as an obstruction to traffic and the tower, described as 'a piece of elegant antiquity', though not the pillar, was moved to the top of Castle Hill, where it can be climbed for a wonderful view of the countryside around. In Gloucester the thirteenth-century market cross was demolished in 1751 'for the better conveniency of carriages'. However, a small late fourteenth-century building known as the Butter Market can be found in a public garden in the city. In Pooley Bridge (Cumbria) the cross was taken down to allow turning space for the coaches and horses bringing visitors to Ullswater. In Denbigh the medieval shaft with eighteenth-century ball finial was replaced by a new version in 1840, which itself had to make way for a war memorial in 1923. Both crosses are still in existence, with the older one occupying a site next to the old town hall. This cross had butchers' stalls attached to it in 1821 and years of knife sharpening have left a number of grooves in the shaft.

Many crosses were defaced or destroyed during the Civil War. An account written at that time in Warwick states: 'on Wednesday the 14th of June, 1642, did Colonel Purefey beat down and deface those monuments of antiquity; and not content with this, they break down the cross in the market place, leaving not one stone upon another, Purefey all the while standing by, animating and encouraging them, until they had finished their so barbarous work'. A few years later, in May 1644, the magnificent cross at Abingdon (Oxfordshire), a faint depiction of which can be found on a side wall of the Long Alley Almshouses, was also totally destroyed by Cromwellian soldiers. In Canterbury (Kent) the puritan mayor destroyed the cross in the Buttermarket and coined farthings from the lead that had covered it, and in London the diarist and author John Evelyn saw 'furious & zelous people demolish the stately crosse in Cheapeside'. Much of this type of damage was the result of the puritans' hatred of religious imagery. For this reason many crosses lost their medieval carved heads, later to be replaced by sundials (the lantern shape was particularly useful for this) or ball finials.

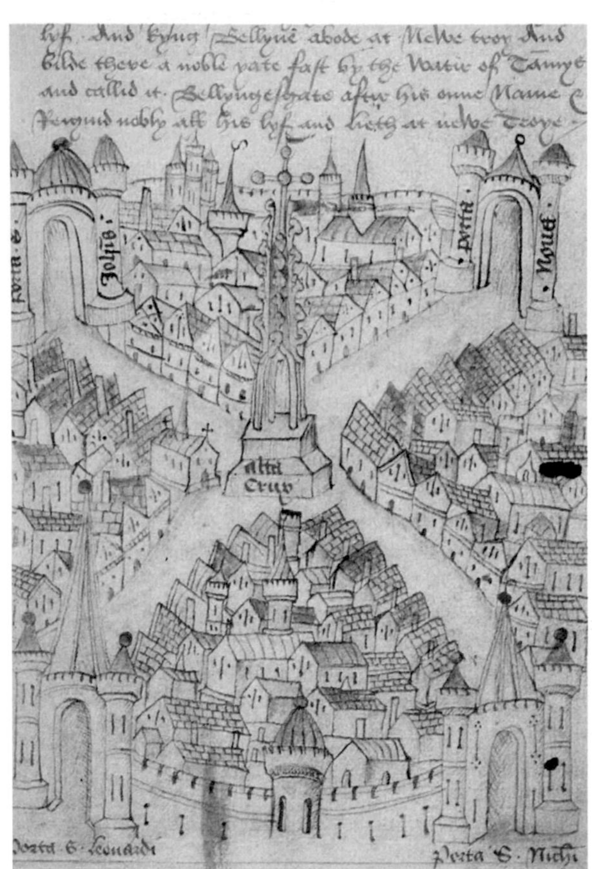

At the centre of medieval Bristol, where High Street, Corn Street, Broad Street and Wine Street meet, stood the painted and gilded High Cross with its niches filled with statues, not of saints, but representing citizens who had contributed to the town's prosperity. (From Ricard's plan for Bristol c. 1479, from The Maire of Bristowe is Kalendar. *By kind permission of Bristol Record office)*

There was another way in which a town could lose its cross. The eighteenth-century love of the picturesque, as well as of the past, in garden design, led to the acquisition of market crosses, redundant or otherwise, by the owners of country estates and other wealthy people. As has already been mentioned, in 1793 Sir John Danvers removed the medieval cross (a shaft with open lantern) from the marketplace in Mountsorrel (Leicestershire) to the grounds of Swithland Hall, replacing it with the Butter Cross. In Cirencester (Gloucestershire) the first Lord Bathurst acquired the town's market cross when, with the help of his friend Alexander Pope, he developed the parkland behind his seat, Cirencester Park. (The cross has since been restored to the town and can be found at the west end of the parish church of St John the Baptist, facing West Market Place.) At Stourhead (Wiltshire) the Bristol High Cross of 1373 (with sixteenth-century additions), given to Henry Hoare in 1764 as the city had no further use for it, still stands in its elevated position near the church. Some of the remains of the fifteenth-century market cross of Chester, knocked down by the puritan army, found their way to the garden of Plas Newydd, where the 'Ladies of Llangollen' placed part of it in front of their home. Similarly, a remnant of the market cross at Wantage (Oxfordshire) was placed 'on a mount' in the garden of J. Stone, who claimed to have been given it by the town and described it in the *Gentleman's Magazine* of February 1796 as 'octagonal, and ... adorned all round with half-length figures of saints or apostles in *alto relieve*'. This cross, given to the town in 1580 by the Earl of Bath, is said to have had the words 'Praie for the good Earls of Bathe, and for the good Master Willm Barnabe, the Beldar [builder] thereof' carved on it. Though not quite like the picture shown in the magazine, and rather curiously shaped, it can be viewed in the Vale and Downland Museum in Wantage. Matters turned out differently for Mr Drummer of Winchester, who in 1770, having bought the market cross from the Paving Commissioners, was stopped from moving it by a crowd of citizens staging a 'small riot', which saved the cross for the city.

An image of the remains of the market cross of Wantage (Oxfordshire) as it appeared in the Gentleman's Magazine *of February 1796.*

Though many market crosses are lost, quite a number have been rescued and restored, even where only part of the original structure has survived. It is as if by holding on to their cross, or what is left of it, a community feels in touch with its history. In Minehead (Somerset) the stump of the old market cross can be found in front of Quirke's Almshouses in Market House Lane, behind the Market House – no longer needed, yet not thrown away. Similarly the base and broken shaft of the butter cross of Scarborough (Yorkshire) is preserved behind railings in West Sandgate. When Corbridge (Northumberland) received its 'remarkable' new cross in 1814, the old one, made up from a Roman capital, a worn medieval shaft with dogtooth carving and an eighteenth-century head, was re-erected near the churchyard. In Chipping Sodbury (Gloucestershire) and Bowden (Scottish Borders) remains of the respective market crosses were incorporated into war memorials after the First World War. In Leicester a High Cross was constructed in 1976, using a column from the sixteenth-century market dome demolished in 1769, to which a ball finial was added. A pillar in front of the former market building of Chipping Norton (Oxfordshire) is made up of the base of a medieval cross and a shaft of the old market hall. Though little is left of the cross in Cleobury Mortimer (Shropshire), its position in the High Street is pointed out in the local history trail. The 'Ca' Steean' (Call Stone), set in the pavement against the town hall in Kendal (Cumbria), is part of the old market cross, from which for many centuries proclamations have been made. In Warkworth (Northumberland) the cross of 1830 is supported by an older stepped base, and in Edinburgh the Mercat Cross, erected in 1885, has remains of a fifteenth-century shaft embedded in it. The Mercat Cross of Stirling, dating to 1891, incorporates the 'puggy', or unicorn, from the structure that was taken down in 1792 as a traffic obstruction, and in Melrose (Scottish Borders) the nineteenth-century restoration includes a mid-seventeenth-century capital with unicorn finial.

Where the market cross has disappeared altogether, its site may still be indicated in some other way, as at Stranraer (Dumfries and Galloway), where three setts in the road in front of the old town hall mark the place. In Perth and Falkirk a circle of cobbles performs the same task. In Cartmel (Cumbria) the market has long gone but the central square is still known as the 'Market Cross and Fish Slabs'.

Elsewhere market crosses have been restored; in the case of Guisborough (Yorkshire) this involved the re-alignment of the sundial at the top. Even complete replacements have been erected, as at Pooley Bridge (Cumbria), where the Millennium Fish Cross, erected in 2000, replaces the one lost earlier. In Mountsorrel (Leicestershire) a copy of the original cross (still standing in the grounds of Swithland Hall) provides an addition to the eighteenth-century Butter Cross. In 1990 the parish council of Eynsham (Oxfordshire) commissioned a replacement for the crumbling remains of the medieval cross. By this time the carvings of 'monastic figures', mentioned by the Honourable John Byng (fifth Viscount Torrington during the last fortnight of his life) in 1785, were no longer visible, and the fragments, dating to *c.* 1350, were held together by a metal framework. The new cross can be seen by the seventeenth-century town and former market hall.

Some market buildings, mothballed in the past because they were considered to be in the way of modern development, have been brought back close to their original sites. This happened in Chippenham (Wiltshire). Here the former butter cross, taken down in 1889 so that a bank could be built in its place, was returned in 1995 from the garden where it had been resited, to be rebuilt in the Market Place. Similarly, the market house and market cross of Bingley (Yorkshire), for years banished to a local park, are back near the site where they belong. In Chester, what was left of the fifteenth-century cross was reconstructed and put in a park. Brought back to its original location, it is once more the place where visitors can listen to announcements made by the town crier.

The town hall of Whitby (Yorkshire), built in 1788, has a stone spiral staircase leading from the centre of the market space beneath to the top floor.

In many towns multi-purpose buildings were erected, providing space not only for market activities but also for the needs of local government. These might include a council chamber, a courtroom and cells, even a space for a fire engine. Some of these buildings are quite small-scale, as at New Buckenham (Norfolk). This village is unique in having preserved its original medieval size and plan. In the former marketplace, which in earlier times contained stalls for shoemakers, butchers, poulterers and fishmongers, stands the Market House, open on three sides at ground level, with Tuscan columns supporting an upper room, once used for the collection of tolls and as a courtroom. In the same county can be found the unusual Market Cross of Wymondham, shaped like an outsize half-timbered dovecot, resting on pillars, and carved with spoons, skewers, tops and spindles as a reminder of the former wood-turning trade of the area. An exterior staircase leads to an upper room, thought to have been used for market court meetings, now housing the local tourist information centre. In Barnard Castle (Durham) the upper floor of the eighteenth-century octagonal market cross, open at ground level, was converted into a courtroom in 1814, with a jury gallery added in 1826. Other examples of small market buildings consisting of one or more rooms on pillars can be found in Princes Risborough (Buckinghamshire), Winster (Derbyshire), Martock (Somerset), Wallingford (Oxfordshire), Wootton Bassett (Wiltshire) – now a museum – and Whitby (Yorkshire), which is unusual in having a stone spiral staircase in the centre of the open market space, leading to the top floor. In Watlington (Oxfordshire) the building, positioned on an island at the junction of three roads, included rooms for the grammar school, similar to the situation in Market Harborough (Leicestershire), already mentioned, and the old market house in Stratford-le-Bow (London), for which a description in *The Mirror* of 1840 reads: 'One of the upper rooms was occupied by Sir John Jolles' school...'

The seventeenth-century market hall formerly standing in the High Street of Titchfield (Hampshire) can now be visited in the Weald and Downland Open Air Museum in Sussex. The ground level of this timber-framed building with brick infill provided space for market activities and a cell, whilst the upper floor was used as a council room. In Tamworth (Staffordshire) Thomas Guy (founder of Guy's Hospital in London) paid for a new town hall, with a market area below, in 1701. This building replaced the two town halls, one for the area of Tamworth lying in Staffordshire and one for the part belonging to Warwickshire, which had recently been pulled down. Built of brick and stone, with high arches, it originally had an outdoor platform from where announcements could be made, and which proved useful at election times. On market days stalls still fill the area, overlooked by a statue of Sir Robert Peel, who in the nineteenth century was MP for the town (as Thomas Guy had been before him). Built entirely of stone is the splendid Market House in the centre of Tetbury (Gloucestershire). Dating to 1655, it was enlarged in 1740 and remodelled in 1816–17, when the hipped roof was installed. It has a cupola with two bells and a weathervane incorporating two gilded dolphins. In 1749 a pump was installed under the arches, paid for by the Reverend J. Wright, and in the nineteenth century a hydrant providing water for steam engines passing through the town was added.

The old market house, Stratford-le-Bow (London), as portrayed in The Mirror of Literature, Amusement, and Instruction *in September 1840.*

The half-timbered Market House on the right, in Ledbury (Herefordshire), was started in 1617 and completed after 1655.

The building had a cell and until 1884 every other Wednesday, 'at 11 o'clock in the forenoon' the magistrates sat in a small room on the upper floor. Even in the twenty-first century a bell is rung to call the town's feoffees (trustees) to their monthly meetings.

Many early market buildings used wood as a major construction material and a number of examples can be found along the Welsh border. Standing on an island at the central crossroads in Llanidloes (Powys) is the only timber-framed market hall in Wales. Built in the early seventeenth century on the site of the old market cross, the former court building is now used for exhibitions. A boulder on the north-west corner is known as the 'Pulpit Stone' as it was used by John Wesley to preach from. A similar market house can be found in Ledbury (Herefordshire), built between 1617 and some time after 1655. The town hall of Bridgnorth (Shropshire), erected

The Market House in Tetbury (Gloucestershire) dates to 1655. It was enlarged in 1740 and remodelled in 1816–17.

just after the Civil War, in 1652, stands in the middle of the High Street. The close-studded upper storey rests on stone arcades enclosing the market area, which is still used for its original purpose. The council chamber and committee room are regularly open to the public. The timber-framed seventeenth-century Market House of Newent (Gloucestershire) rests on twelve wooden posts and has an outside staircase leading to a large room now used as a local history museum.

The County Hall in Abingdon (Oxfordshire), with a market area beneath, was built between 1678 and 1682 by one of Christopher Wren's London masons. Celia Fiennes described it as 'the finest in England' in 1694.

The Old Market Hall in Shrewsbury (Shropshire), dating to 1595–6, has been described as 'an unusually stately late Elizabethan public building'. Unlike many early town halls, it is built of stone. The statue of a man in armour in the centre light of the upper window formerly stood on the medieval Welsh Bridge, which was taken down in 1791. The market hall of Faversham (Kent) was built in 1574, at the instigation of the citizens of the town and those of thirteen nearby parishes. In 1603 it was converted into a guildhall (later enlarged and altered) with a market area underneath, which is still used by stallholders three times a week. It is distinguished by its clock tower with an octagonal cupola and a weathervane in the form of a golden dragon with a forked tail. The County Hall in Abingdon (Oxfordshire) was built between 1678 and 1682 (when Abingdon was the county town of Berkshire) by Christopher Kempster, one of Christopher Wren's London masons, and remains much as Celia Fiennes described it c. 1694: 'the Market Cross is the finest in England, its all of free stone and very lofty, even the Isles or Walk below is a lofty arch on severall pillars of square stone and four square pillars, over it are large Roomes with handsome Windows.' The basement was used as a warehouse, the ground floor for market activities and the first floor as a courtroom for the county assizes. It is now a museum and on special occasions buns are thrown to the crowds in the marketplace below – a custom that started with the coronation of George III in 1760.

Less grand, though still imposing, is the Guildhall of High Wycombe (Buckinghamshire). Built in 1757 as the 'Great Market House' and town hall, it is

View of Faversham, Kent, 1832; engraving after Thomas Mann Baynes (1794–1854). (Private Collection / The Bridgeman Art Library.)

situated diagonally opposite the Little Market House or 'Pepperpot', designed by Robert Adam in 1761 to rehouse the shambles and butter market. For the convenience of travellers, an inscription on the latter building states: 'To London 29 miles' and 'To Oxford 25 miles'. On market days both buildings are surrounded by stalls, with some of these occupying the open space under the Guildhall. In contrast, the market house (which had a corn loft over it) of Tring (Hertfordshire) was described in 1819 as 'a mean edifice on wooden pillars having a pillory and cage [lock-up] underneath'. It was demolished in 1900 and replaced by a new building provided by the Rothschild family.

It can be observed that over time a number of former market houses have had their arches filled in, with the enclosed space put to various uses. One example is the sixteenth-century Moot Hall in Aldeburgh (Suffolk), its name indicating that this was a meeting place, used for debate. Though part of it is now used as a museum, the building is still the town hall (scene of the opening of Benjamin Britten's opera *Peter Grimes*). Now fully enclosed, the north end originally was open for the use of market traders, whilst the south end contained prison cells. A rather decorative example is the Market House in Rothwell (Northamptonshire), built for Sir Thomas Tresham. Started in 1578, it took more than three hundred years to complete. The frieze above the first floor contains ninety coats of arms, including those of landowners of Rothwell Hundred and other Northamptonshire families. Other examples of enclosed former market buildings are the early seventeenth-century market hall, now a tourist information centre, in Bakewell (Derbyshire) and the town halls of Brackley (Northamptonshire), built in 1706 for the first Duke of Bridgewater, Kelso (Scottish Borders), erected in 1816, and Chipping Norton (Oxfordshire), dating to 1842. In Leominster (Herefordshire) the splendid Old Town Hall, built by the King's Carpenter, John Abel, in 1633, was moved from the town centre to a local park, where it serves as offices. Its inscription reads: '*Vive deo gratus, Toti mundo tumulatus, Crimine mundatus, Semper transire paratus.* Where Justice rule, there vertu flow. *Vive ut post vivas. Sat cito si sat bene.* Like columns do upprop the fabrik of a building, so noble gentri dos support the honor of a Kingdom. *In memoria aeterna erit Justus.*' In Cornmarket, Wimborne Minster (Dorset), stands the red-brick market house that

The Guildhall or 'Great Market House' (left), built in 1757, and the Little Market House or 'Pepperpot' (right), designed by Robert Adam in 1761 to house the shambles and the butter market in High Wycombe (Buckinghamshire).

The market house with corn loft in Tring (Hertfordshire). In 1819 it was described as 'a mean edifice on wooden pillars, having a pillory and cage underneath'. It was demolished in 1900. (By kind permission of Mike Bass.)

was built in 1758 'with the assistance of the Neighbouring Gentlemen by the FRIENDLY SOCIETY of this Town', according to a commemorative plaque. There, on the site of the former guildhall, corn, wool and other commodities were sold, the official weights and measures kept and market offences dealt with.

In Northern Ireland many towns feature market buildings with courtrooms on the upper floor. In The Square, Hillsborough (Down), is the former market house, now the tourist information office, which in 1810 had a courtroom added to it. No longer used as such, it is occasionally open to the public. The former market and court house of Cushendall (Antrim), built in 1858, can now be found in the Ulster Folk and Transport Museum. Here the left-hand door leads to the former market hall with its stalls, whilst the right-hand door gives access to the court upstairs, where the interior includes a raised bench for the magistrates and the tables and chairs used by the clerks, solicitors and witnesses. The accused sat on a chair near the window. On the ground floor is a cell where defendants awaited trial or a transfer to prison, if found guilty. The building was set back from the road so that there was room for stock pens for the livestock that was regularly sold there. The Market House in The Square in Ballynahinch (Down) was completed in 1795 for the Earl of Moira, as an amenity for the town his family had developed. The market hall was reached through ground-floor arches that were tall enough to allow a cart to back in for loading and unloading in wet weather. The first floor housed an assembly room for meetings and entertainment and a small Jury Room, where courts were held. It had a clock added in 1841. It is now used as a community centre.

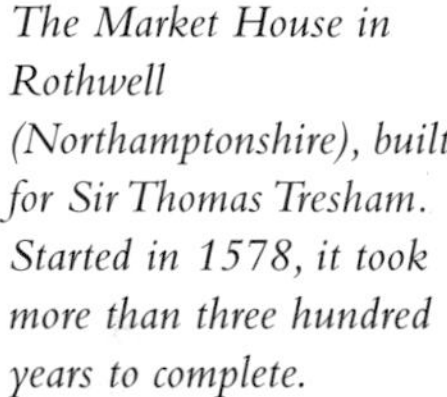

The Market House in Rothwell (Northamptonshire), built for Sir Thomas Tresham. Started in 1578, it took more than three hundred years to complete.

Chapter Four

CORN MARKETS AND CORN EXCHANGES

> HERE is a good Market Cross well carv'd and a large Market House on pillars for the corn...

(Celia Fiennes describing Taunton, Somerset, in 1697)

CORN MARKETS have always been important, dealing as they do in a staple commodity. Both Celia Fiennes and Daniel Defoe, travelling through Britain at the end of the seventeenth century and in the early eighteenth, mentioned grain regularly in their descriptions of the countryside and the towns they visited. The former observed how in Devon the narrow lanes obliged farmers to 'carry their Corn [to market] ... on horses backes with frames of wood like pannyers on either side the horse, so load it high and tye it with cords'. The latter, amongst other references to corn dealing, described Farnham (Surrey) as 'without exception the greatest corn-market in England, London excepted; that is to say, particularly for wheat, of which so vast a quantity is brought every market-day to this market, that a gentleman told me, he once counted on a market-day eleven hundred teams of horse, all drawing wagons or carts, loaden with wheat at this market; every team of which is supposed to bring what they call a load, that is to say, forty bushel of wheat to market; which is in the whole, four and forty thousand bushel...' (A bushel, equivalent to just 8 gallons – the largest measure available – was commonly used for corn.) The importance of corn markets may be indicated by a milestone on the road leading out of Winchester (Hampshire) to nearby Romsey which gives the distance as '10M of 1CH [10 miles less 1 chain] to Corn Exchange' of that town – a helpful guide to travelling market traders and farmers.

As was the case with other merchandise, a particular area of a town would be allocated to the sale of corn. Sometimes we are reminded of this by a street name that records the trade formerly carried out in the area: Cornhill (Dorchester, Dorset; Ottery St Mary, Devon; Ipswich, Suffolk), Corn Market (Bakewell, Derbyshire, and Faringdon, Oxfordshire), Corn Exchange Street (Cambridge), Cornmarket Street (Oxford), Mealmarket (Hexham, Northumberland) and Oatmeal Row (Salisbury, Wiltshire) amongst others. Some towns, including Scarborough (Yorkshire) and Melton Mowbray (Leicestershire), had a corn cross around which dealers did business. The latter also had a Corn Wall, last mentioned in 1814, which is thought to have been a permanent stall where corn was displayed. Though a lot of business happened in the open air, sometimes a building might provide shelter, as was the case in Canterbury (Kent), where until 1824 the corn market took place in St Andrew's Church. Sometimes purpose-built structures were made available. A plan of Kingsbridge (Devon), painted on vellum and dating to 1586,

OPPOSITE
Traders bringing samples of grain to the London corn exchange, Mark Lane. (By kind permission of the Museum of English Rural Life, Reading University)

RIGHT
Detail of a sheaf of corn on the Corn Exchange, Swaffham (Norfolk).

BELOW
The reconstructed Corn Cross in Melton Mowbray (Leicestershire). The original cross around which the corn market was held stood in the centre of the street.

shows the former single-storeyed corn market, describing it as 'The trewe Platt of the newe byldyng, upon five pyllers of stone…' (This structure was turned into butchers' shambles at the end of the eighteenth century and as such has already been referred to.) In the same county the Old Market House of Tiverton, its wooden Tuscan pillars fronting an open ground floor, was built as a corn market in 1699 and rebuilt after a fire in 1731. Also in that period the Corn Exchange of Rochester (Kent) was erected, opening in 1706 – a gift of Sir Cloudesley Shovel, MP for the city. Only the façade is left but its enormous clock makes an interesting landmark.

There were two ways in which farmers and dealers – millers, maltsters and corn merchants – wanting to buy and sell corn publicly might choose to do business: either they made use of a 'pitched' market or they resorted to a sample market. With the former method, the entire amount of grain to be sold would be brought to market in sacks. Representing the full load, one bag would be displayed in the marketplace so that prospective buyers could check the quality of its contents; the rest would stay on the cart stored in one of the inn-yards of the town. This meant that if a buyer had any doubt he could inspect the rest of the load before a deal was struck.

Most pitch markets took place in the open air, with sacks displayed directly on the pavement, maybe on a bed of straw. There were pitch markets in Warminster (described by Celia Fiennes as 'a pretty little town a good market for corn'), Devizes, Salisbury (all in Wiltshire) and Yeovil (Somerset). In Wigton (Cumbria) the corn market was held near St Mary's Church. Its site is marked by cobbles forming the letters W, B and O in the pavement, indicating the areas where wheat, barley and oats were sold.

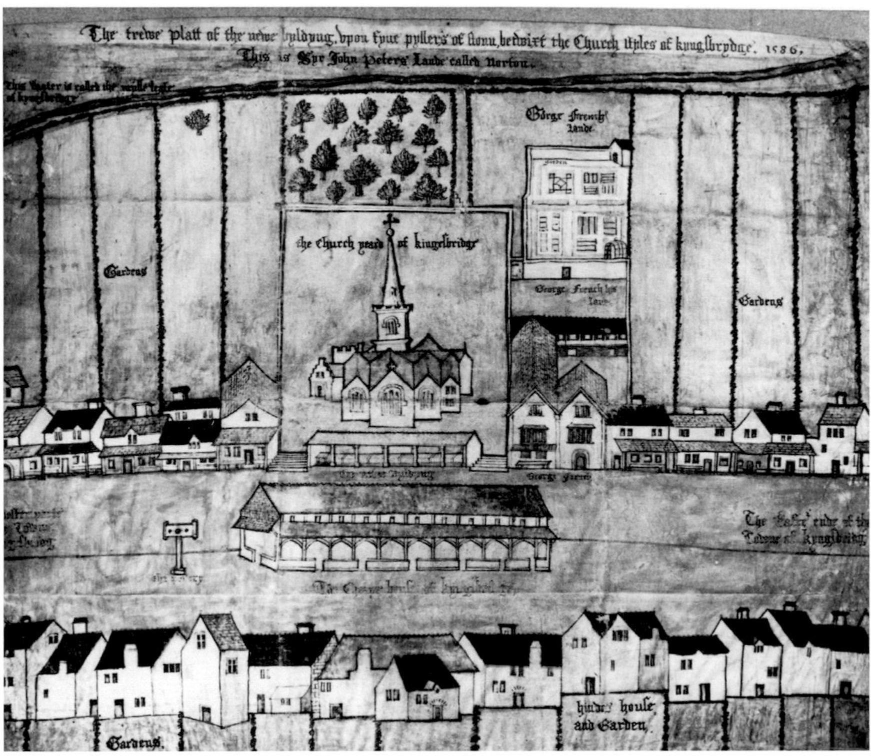

An engraving of 1819 of the 1586 Platt of Kingsbridge (Devon), showing 'the newe byldyng, upon five pyllers of stone betwixt the Church styles of Kyngsbrydge', i.e. the single-storey corn market behind 'The Cheape house'. Note the pillory to the left of 'The Cheape' (market) house. (Courtesy of Cookworthy Museum, Kingsbridge, Devon)

Lincoln's corn market took place on Steep Hill until in 1847 it was moved to the new corn exchange in Cornhill, where later yet another exchange was established.

Sometimes corn dealers were able to find shelter from bad weather under the cover of the local market building, as happened in High Wycombe (Buckinghamshire), where the area under the Guildhall (or 'Great Market Hall' as it was sometimes known) was used for this purpose. The street running in front of it is still called 'Corn Market'. In the same way the open ground floor of the Old Market House in Shrewsbury (Shropshire) provided some protection against bad weather. In Tetbury (Gloucestershire) the corn market was held under the iron veranda of the White Hart inn (now the Snooty Fox hotel) until the upper floor of the Market House was vacated by the wool trade in the early eighteenth century and turned into a corn exchange. The Market House of Castle Cary (Somerset), built in 1856, provided a pitch area on the open ground floor and a room on the first floor where (it has been suggested) samples drawn from sacks pulled up through the trapdoor (which still exists) could be shown on ledges lining the walls underneath the windows. When the building was first opened it was decided that 'Tolls for corn' should be 'as at Shepton [Mallet, Somerset]', with the exception that, instead of the farmer paying 1s. per wagon, he was charged the same for every sample, but nothing for unloading a wagon. In Uxbridge (Middlesex) a pitch market was held on the open ground floor of the market house that was built in 1789. The upper floor, supported on wooden Tuscan columns, and surmounted by a clock turret, was used as a corn exchange. In Princes Risborough (Buckinghamshire) the Market House was rebuilt as a corn market in 1867.

The Market House in Castle Cary (Somerset), built in 1856, had a pitch market on the open ground floor and a room on the first floor where corn samples were shown.

Where outdoor trading took place, deals were often sealed in a nearby hostelry, a place that was sometimes preferred even where a corn exchange had been built. In Brigg (Lincolnshire) it was noticeable how on market days, right up to the 1950s, the mid nineteenth-century corn exchange was almost empty whilst the pub next door was crowded with traders. When in 1793 the market house of Lewes (Sussex) was pulled down, corn trading was transferred to the Star inn (converted into the town hall in 1893).

The alternative was dealing by sample, again often in a local public house. (By tradition all kinds of business were concluded in inns.) This involved farmers carrying small bags of the grain types they wanted to sell, so enabling buyers to decide if the quality was right for their requirements. In this way matters were simplified, with farmers travelling light, and therefore faster and more cheaply, as no cart, horses or assistants (for the lifting of bags) were needed. The dealer would receive his purchase straight from the farm. It even became possible to delegate the task of selling from sample, with pub landlords taking on the job on commission. In Stow-on-the-Wold (Gloucestershire) transactions took place in the Talbot, facing the Market Square. Here any farmer unable to attend in person could post his samples through the brass letterbox marked 'FOR CORN RETURNS', still in place. However, many people, Daniel Defoe amongst them, were opposed to this method, feeling that it could lead to deception.

Though in a number of towns outdoor trading continued well into the twentieth century (in Scarborough, Yorkshire, it went on until the 1950s), in many places indoor facilities started to be provided, often in the town hall, or in an extension to it. In Halstead (Essex) the ground floor of the town hall, built on Market Hill in 1850, was used as a corn exchange until in 1865 a purpose-built replacement (now the library) took over. In the centre of the triangular marketplace of Woodbridge (Suffolk), the striking Shire Hall with its Dutch gables (given by Thomas Seckford in 1575), had an open ground floor (enclosed in 1803) with arches big enough to allow carts to pass through. This area was used as a corn market until just before the Second World War. In Chichester (Sussex) the Council House, built in 1731, included a corn market – a fact recorded on a stone panel in the council chamber. In Chard (Somerset) the town hall of 1834 had a corn exchange (since replaced) added in 1883. A similar development took place in Blandford Forum (Dorset), where the corn exchange can be reached via the shambles underneath the town hall. The corn exchange of Swindon Old Town (as distinct from the later New Town, developed in response to the establishment of the Great Western Railway's locomotive works there) was built next to the town hall in 1866, complete with a glass-domed triangular market hall and an 80-foot tower. In Penzance (Cornwall) the corn exchange was housed in the centrally located, domed market house, which included the guildhall. (The building is now a bank with shops underneath.) In 1865 Towcester (Northamptonshire), too, combined its new town hall with a corn exchange, as did Ipswich (Suffolk) in 1882.

The letter box marked 'FOR CORN RETURNS' in the wall of the Talbot in Stow-on-the-Wold (Gloucestershire), where traders could post their grain samples.

In some places a corn exchange was joined to an existing market building. This happened in Doncaster (Yorkshire), where in 1873 the market hall of 1847–9 was added to in this way. Similarly, the Pannier Market in Barnstaple (Devon), built in 1855–6 behind the Guildhall and courtroom, was extended with the addition of a corn exchange in 1864. In Bideford (Devon) the Pannier Market of 1884 was

The former corn exchange at Halstead (Essex), built in 1865, is now a library.

constructed to house the meat shambles, the fish market and the corn exchange, and in Kirkby Lonsdale (Cumbria) the weekly corn market took place in the Market House, built in 1854. In Bristol a corn exchange was fashioned from the Gloucestershire Market Hall, standing behind the elder John Wood's Exchange in Corn Street, *c.* 1813.

Elsewhere, new buildings, combining a town hall with a corn exchange, were erected. This was the case in Wareham (Dorset), where the town hall of 1869–70 included a corn exchange. In the same county Dorchester's new town hall, built in 1847–8, included a corn exchange on the ground floor and had a police station at the back. Five years after the opening of Leicester's corn exchange in 1850 an upper floor was added for magistrates' offices, which could be reached via a combined staircase and bridge. These various combinations reinforce the point made before about the way in which the functions of local government, the judicial system and markets often were intertwined.

As the population increased and towns expanded during the period of the Industrial Revolution, more corn was grown and markets specialising in this commodity grew in importance. Those on easy routes to London, other major cities and densely populated areas like the Midlands did especially well. In Scotland, Dalkeith (Midlothian) had an important grain market, as had Haddington (East Lothian), which in *John Bartholomew's Gazetteer of the British Isles* for 1887 was described as 'one of the largest' in that country. As a result of the increased business opportunities in many cities, groups of shareholders, realising the potential profits this situation offered, combined to erect often quite splendid corn exchanges, some of which might outdo a town's older civic buildings. In King's Lynn (Norfolk) the market house in Tuesday Market was pulled down to make way for a grand new corn exchange. From the beginning, many of these prestigious structures were erected with the additional aim of providing a venue where people could be entertained at times when dealing was not taking place.

Proceedings did not always go smoothly. In Dereham (formerly East Dereham, Norfolk) the East Dereham Corn Exchange Company was set up by a group of prominent local men, including the Earl of Leicester, Lord Hastings, Lord Sondes, Lord Suffield and Captain Adlington, with the aim of providing the town with a corn exchange in the Market Place. However, from the beginning problems were encountered with the site earmarked by the company, as this was owned by several individuals (including various proprietors of the butchers' stalls), who needed to be bought out. When the substantial building, topped by a statue of the agricultural improver Coke of Norfolk, had been erected in 1857, disputes arose about the perceived loss of a public right of way, ending in the Vice-Chancellor's Court. However, the opposition, led by the rival East Dereham Corn Market Company, lost and the final judgement was celebrated with 'the joyous ringing of the church bells'. The building cost £18,000.

When in 1868 Cambridge Council decided to replace the town's existing corn exchange, built in 1842 on St Andrew's Hill, it also faced criticism. A local draper, Robert Sayle, questioned the right of the local authorities to spend money meant for the improvement of the marketplace on a new building, taking his case all the way to the House of Lords, though to no avail. The site, in the present Corn Exchange Lane, was bought for £5,000 and architectural designs were invited for submission. The contract, allowing the builder, William Elworthy, to spend £5,276, was signed on 1 December 1873 and on 6 November 1875 the building was opened with a civic procession from the Guildhall, followed by a dinner for local dignitaries, during which the mayor stated that 'it was a building worthy of the borough'. Two days later, the celebrations were continued with a promenade concert, when an unfortunate mistake was made during the national anthem, leading to an attack on the mayor's house. The court case that followed brought reporters and general sightseers from far and wide, making it difficult for the corn traders to do business. In 1965 the building closed, to be refurbished for entertainment purposes only, and a new corn exchange was built at the cattle market, costing £9,000.

Throughout the nineteenth century architects were engaged to design buildings of which local communities could be proud, with a certain amount of rivalry between towns. Architecturally, many were inspired by classical styles, constructing virtual temples to corn, with quite a number featuring a figure of Ceres, Roman goddess of the harvest. Examples can be found in Newark-on-Trent (Nottinghamshire), King's Lynn (Norfolk), Devizes (Wiltshire) and Tunbridge Wells (Kent), at the last gracing a building that had been converted from a theatre. Another can be found on top of the classical façade of the corn exchange built in 1857 in Cornhill, Banbury (Oxfordshire). In this town a rival exchange, located diagonally opposite in the neighbouring Market Place, dates from the same year. However, its façade was changed *c.* 1880, favouring the French Renaissance style, including a relief of the sun in splendour and corn sheaves. (In spite of these two rather grand buildings, it was said that most business was carried out in the Red Lion.)

Statue of Ceres on the roof of the former corn exchange built in 1857 in Devizes (Wiltshire).

Generally ornamentation involved a number of variations on the theme of agriculture. Wheat sheaves and cornucopias were particularly popular. Examples of the former can be found in Attleborough, Swaffham (both in Norfolk) and Halstead (Essex). In Cirencester (Gloucestershire) a cornucopia enhances the façade above the entrance gate (incorporating wheat sheaves) leading to the Corn Hall. Further decorations include garlands, wheat ears, flowers and fruit. In Newark-on-Trent (Nottinghamshire) the corn is held by a female figure, complemented by another one in charge of a cornucopia. The façade is further decorated with corn motifs. In Sudbury (Suffolk) each of the four giant pillars is crowned with a sheaf of corn. The Corn Exchange in Cambridge has panels showing rural scenes, including one depicting the reaping and binding of corn. The pediment of the Corn Exchange in Romsey (Hampshire) displays agricultural tools, as well as the ubiquitous stacks of wheat. In Oxfordshire Witney's Corn Exchange of 1863, replacing the Tudor corn returns office, has a display of fruit. The pediment of the Corn

Exchange in Bury St Edmunds (Suffolk), built in 1861–2, shows a male figure with cattle, a plough and a spade opposite a female figure with a sheaf of corn and baskets of fruit and vegetables. Underneath is the statement 'THE EARTH IS THE LORD'S AND THE FULNESS THEREOF'. A band of carved millstones surrounds the exterior of the very grand Corn Exchange in Leeds (Yorkshire), a large oval building, described in the Pevsner Architectural Guide as 'of national, maybe international importance'. The clock inside is flanked by wheat sheaves.

Imposing porticoes, pillars of the giant order and large pediments were regularly used to emphasise the importance of a building. In Chichester (Sussex) the Greek Doric portico of the Corn Exchange (built in 1832 to replace the eighteenth-century facilities in the Council House mentioned before) spans the pavement. The corn exchanges of New Malton (Yorkshire), Bishop's Stortford (Hertfordshire), Northampton and Sudbury (Suffolk) all use the giant order with Tuscan columns, which in Worcester are described as 'truly colossal'.

The Italianate style was also very popular and examples of corn exchanges using it can be found in Newbury (Berkshire), Alcester (Warwickshire), Louth (Lincolnshire), Wallingford (Oxfordshire) and Melton Mowbray (Leicestershire), the last crowned by a wooden turret. Other styles employed include references to the Jacobean period, as in Melrose (Scottish Borders), Spalding (Lincolnshire) and Worksop (Nottinghamshire), where the building has been erected in an Italianate/Jacobean manner. In Oxford, Leominster (Herefordshire) and Faringdon (Oxfordshire) the Gothic style was favoured, and in Lichfield (Staffordshire) the architect of the combined savings bank, Market Hall (for the use of butter and poultry sellers) and Corn Exchange looked to the Tudor period. (In this city corn tolls had been abolished in 1741, the result of a gift by one of its MPs.) Various forms of Renaissance-inspired architecture were used in Haverhill (Suffolk), Beverley (here the red-brick and terracotta building included the public

The Corn Exchange in Sudbury (Suffolk) was built in 1841. The four giant Tuscan columns support sheaves of corn. Note also the group of reapers at rest above the façade.

The oval Corn Exchange in Leeds was built in 1860–2.

swimming pool) and Doncaster (both in Yorkshire). The Corn Exchange of Dalkeith (Midlothian), once Scotland's largest indoor grain market, has twin gables, one on either side of a bell turret. In Dorchester (Dorset) an ornate clock tower was added on one corner of the Corn Exchange, partly paid for by Alderman Galpin. As it lacked footings,

The Corn Exchange and Market Hall (and savings bank on the left) in Lichfield (Staffordshire). (From the Illustrated London News, *12 January 1850.)*

the town's inhabitants waited for its imminent collapse and it became known as 'Galpin's Folly' (but so far it has held out). In contrast to some of the rather grand buildings mentioned, the Corn Exchange of Bath, situated away from the city centre in Walcot Street, is somewhat plain and narrow.

As we have already seen, the opening of a new corn exchange was often treated as a special occasion. In Lichfield (Staffordshire) the president of the company in charge of the building led his guests up the wide set of stone steps to the large room (63 feet in length and 30 feet wide, with a capacity of between six and eight hundred people) for a great dinner underneath three magnificent chandeliers. In Swindon a procession, headed by a brass band, made its way up the hill from the Goddard Arms to the new building, where an official dinner and ball were enjoyed. In contrast, guests attending the opening of the corn exchange in Plymouth (Devon) were treated to a cold luncheon, for which privilege they were expected to pay 2s. 6d. This was followed by the official opening by the mayor, who was presented with a silver key to unlock the gates.

Usually business would be conducted once or twice a week for a few hours at a time. When, rather late compared to many other towns, Plymouth decided in 1893 to put a corn exchange over the entrance of the early nineteenth-century market complex, it was planned for it to open on Thursdays only.

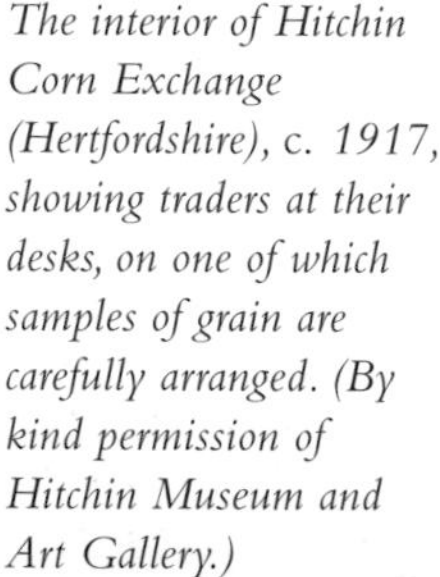

The interior of Hitchin Corn Exchange (Hertfordshire), c. 1917, showing traders at their desks, on one of which samples of grain are carefully arranged. (By kind permission of Hitchin Museum and Art Gallery.)

However, soon Tuesdays were added. The opening hours were from 1 to 4 p.m., with a bell announcing closure of business. In the beginning farmers offering corn samples paid 1s. for a day ticket but this soon rose to 2s. One of the rules stated that smoking was forbidden.

One of the twelve mid nineteenth-century corn dealers' desks, paid for by the feoffees of Tetbury (Gloucestershire), for the upper room of the Market House.

Within the corn exchange, dealers would meet in a room filled with desks for the display of samples and the conclusion of business deals. When a room in the Market House of Tetbury (Gloucestershire) was converted into a grain market around 1860, the feoffees paid for twelve tables and desktops to be made for this purpose, six of which still exist. At the same time two extra windows were inserted. Lighting was of great importance, as is demonstrated in a photograph dating to the beginning of the twentieth century showing the interior of Hitchin (Hertfordshire) Corn Exchange, lit from above. The lantern roof of the corn exchange in Hadleigh (Suffolk), described as 'a handsome building' in *A Topographical Dictionary of England* in 1848, also provides excellent visibility inside. In 1848 *White's Directory* for Romford (Essex) stated that the corn exchange had fifty-four stands, 'lighted from the roof'. Equally, the glazing in the former corn exchange of Kelso (Scottish Borders) enabled the seventy-one stalls inside to be lit appropriately. In Leeds the elliptical oculus of the Corn Exchange was designed to increase the natural lighting, and in Bishop's Stortford (Hertfordshire) the statue of Ceres on top of the 1828 building was later removed to allow a circular glass roof to be installed, giving the sixty-five people trading

The elliptical oculus of Leeds Corn Exchange increases the natural light.

inside the extra light they required. However, not all traders were looked after so well, for in 1869 the *Northampton Mercury* wrote of the 'miserable lighting' in the local corn exchange, saying that it could be described only as that of 'a congregation of gossiping new moons in a fog'.

By law regular corn returns had to be made to specially appointed inspectors. The figures collected in this way helped towards the regulation of imports and exports of corn and towards a calculation of the average price of corn. Inside the Butter Cross in Barnard Castle (Durham) the following notice can be found:

CORN RETURNS
TOWN OF BARNARD CASTLE
Notice – The place appointed for making and
delivering Corn Returns within this Town is the
Inland Revenue Office. Hall Street where an Excise
Officer will attend as Inspector of Corn Returns on
the days on which such accounts or returns are
required by law to be made.

At the end of the nineteenth century farming went through a period of decline and corn exchanges lost business, with some companies going bankrupt. However, a number did survive and the last corn exchange to close its doors to the business for which it had been built was the restrained neo-classical building in Diss (Norfolk), at the end of the twentieth century. As already mentioned, from the beginning many corn exchanges had been built with rooms suitable for meetings, lectures, even libraries (in Much Wenlock, Shropshire, an agricultural library was included at the instigation of Dr William Penny Brookes, in an effort to combat the town's failing economy) and various kinds of entertainment, including musical and theatrical performances. A substantial number have continued in this role, whilst others now function as shopping centres or restaurants. As a result these buildings have not been lost to the townscape and are still there to interest and delight the passer-by.

BARGAIN STONES

In front of the Exchange in Corn Street, Bristol, which replaced the earlier old Tolzey Market by All Saints' Church, four brass pillars can be found, measuring about 3 feet in height and approximately 2 feet in diameter. Dating to the sixteenth and seventeenth centuries, these are known as 'nails' and were used by merchants to conclude business deals. It is said that farmers would do this by placing a sample of corn on the 'nail' and, once a price was agreed, the merchant placing his order would pay the full amount in advance of delivery. From this derives the saying 'paying on the nail', though its meaning has changed from paying in advance to paying promptly. 'Nails' can also be found at the Liverpool Exchange and in the Victorian covered market at Bath, where the eighteenth-century pillar has a slate top. It has been suggested that special places for payment may have existed at least since Saxon times. It is thought that the large rock

One of four 'nails' found in front of the Exchange in Corn Street, Bristol. Here business deals were concluded, leading to the expression 'paying on the nail'.

The 'Free Trade Loaf' on the Great Orme (Conwy). It is thought that this large rock was the place where trade arrangements were finalised.

known as the 'Free Trade Loaf' on the Great Orme (Conwy) was the place where contracts were sealed and bargains literally struck. In eighteenth-century Doune (Stirling) a standing stone (locally known as the 'Deil's Heid'), believed to date from the Bronze Age, was used in the same way. At one corner of the sixteenth-century Market Hall in Pembridge (Herefordshire) two stones known as 'nails' can be observed, and St Peter's churchyard in Wolverhampton contains the 'Bargain Stone', where, it is said, deals were sealed by a handshake through the opening in the middle.

BELOW LEFT
At one corner of the sixteenth-century Market Hall in Pembridge (Herefordshire) two stones known as 'nails' can be found.

BELOW
The Bargain Stone in St Peter's churchyard, Wolverhampton. It is said that traders shook hands through the opening in the middle to confirm an agreement.

NEW FLOWER MARKET, COVENT GARDEN, IN COURSE OF CONSTRUCTION.

Chapter Five

AN AGE OF IMPROVEMENT

'A BETTER market or worse accommodation rarely shall we see,' wrote one commentator in 1806 of the Pannier Market at Barnstaple (Devon) before the local authorities had provided the town with the present, much admired market building.

From the end of the eighteenth century the population of Britain started to increase sharply. This, combined with the invention and harnessing of steam power (allowing factories to be built in urban areas rather than near fast-flowing rivers in the country), brought about a huge increase in the size of many towns. As a new and expanding workforce moved in, the nature of many places changed. The ways of the small pre-industrial market town soon were no longer adequate in the developing conurbations and for various reasons market arrangements and practices were altered. Of great importance was the introduction of the Municipal Corporations Act in 1835, which established the principle of local authorities, elected by ratepayers, replacing the self-appointed cliques hitherto in charge of many towns. These new authorities were empowered to levy rates for improvements in the environment and this arrangement helped towards the development of a civic pride that often found expression in the cleaning up of city centres, including market provision. Of further help in this were the Public Health Act and Nuisance Removal Act, both passed in 1848 and the result of a better understanding of the importance of hygiene. All this led to a general clearing of streets, with markets relegated to specific, self-contained areas and halls.

The construction of grand municipal buildings, including covered markets, helped to proclaim a town's success, wealth and progress and in this respect cities might well try to outdo each other, much as they did in the building of a corn exchange. Clocks and fountains were much in evidence. At the same time many newly wealthy manufacturers liked to see their names connected with prestigious projects. The latest manufacturing processes and up-to-date construction methods meant that cast iron, steel and glass became important components in the new buildings, contributing to changes in style as well as to increased cleanliness. Improved conditions did not only take place in the large new conurbations but many smaller towns followed suit, though on a lesser scale. As a result the new trends in environmental sanitation meant that as the nineteenth century progressed many residents saw their surroundings change for the better.

As outdoor market stalls came to be regarded as sources of clutter and street fouling, in many places these might be moved to special trading areas – often slightly away from the centre – where dealers could more easily be kept an eye on. This happened in Oxford, where, as a result of the Mileways Act of 1771 (passed by a committee consisting of six members of the university and six members of the town council), a new market was provided in 1774 between High Street and Market Street

OPPOSITE
The Flower Market, Covent Garden, in 1872. A board still in evidence today states that the rates for 'The Flower Stands' were 'after the rate of one shilling and eight pence per annum for every squarefoot superficial of such stand.'

by the Paving Commission. At first only the messier stalls – those belonging to butchers and fishmongers – were relocated but these were later joined by the fruit and vegetable mongers and dairy salesmen, all to be supervised by a beadle. At about the same time, in 1775, the city of Bath, too, had a new market designed for it. After a visit to Oxford in July 1785 the Honourable John Byng wrote in his diary that he had been taken by an acquaintance, Mr Reynolds, 'to admire their new market, which he [Reynolds] said was productive of every luxury; tho' [in the opinion of Byng] both in building and product it appear'd very inferior to that of Bath'. In the nineteenth century both markets were rebuilt. In Bath this happened between 1861 and 1863, when a twelve-sided dome was constructed over the centre of the building. Oxford waited till the 1890s for the restructuring and covering over of its market. One wonders how John Byng would have judged these reincarnations? As we shall see, where market provisions were successful these would repeatedly be improved and enlarged.

In eighteenth-century Glasgow, too, the authorities made attempts to clear the streets of market activities, doing so by allocating designated, partially roofed and enclosed areas to particular trades, including a green and potato market in Candleriggs, a fruit market in Bell's Wynd (where they were joined by country butchers) and separate beef and mutton markets in King Street. The fish market, with its lead-covered

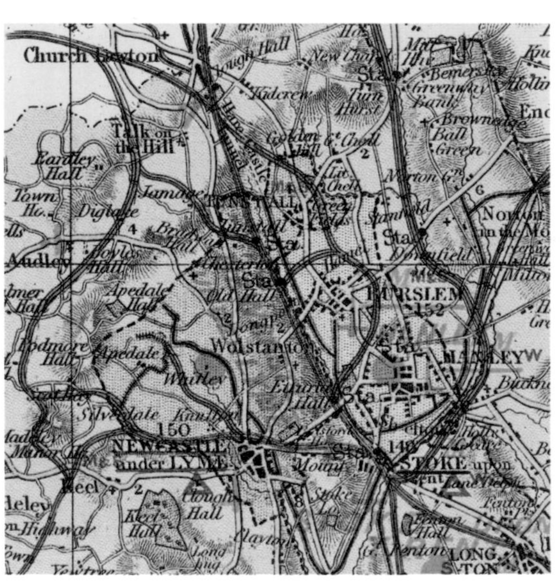

BELOW
A map of Staffordshire; dating to 1884, it shows the days on which markets were held in the various towns shown, indicated by letters in blue (e.g. 'w' for Wednesday)

tables and running water, was said to be the 'completest of their kind in Britain'. Yet not every market building was successful. In Hove (Sussex) the Old Market, built in 1828 for the area known as Brunswick Town, failed almost immediately as both stallholders and customers preferred the rival new market next to Brighton town hall. It is now a centre for the arts, education and the community.

As was the case in other expanding towns, Liverpool had a number of general markets, each serving a different part of the growing town. St John's Market was opened by the corporation in 1822. It was brick-built and had eight entrances and 136 windows. The five avenues inside were lined with 404 stalls and fifty-eight shops. In the beginning it was 'brightly illuminated' every night by 144 gaslights. Before it was demolished in 1963, it was popular because on Saturdays farmers came in with fresh produce. St James's Market, serving the south side of the town, was added in 1827, and St Martin's Market in 1829. The last had deteriorated into 'the dirtiest, the dreariest and the dingiest of the town's markets' by 1889.

In Cardiff most market activity was centred in and around the Guildhall in High Street and in its continuation, St Mary Street. The mess created by the stallholders obliged the street commissioners to impose the rule that traders should leave the pavement clear of rubbish so that on Sundays people could walk unhindered to church. The first covered market was built privately in 1822, to be superseded in 1835 by a municipal one, containing 349 stalls and a mixture of open counters and lock-ups arranged in four aisles and along the balcony, which was reserved for non-food traders. The market superintendent was given a raised office, surmounted by a clock tower. This market was replaced in 1884 by a five-storey market hall, which in turn made way for yet another reincarnation, built by the borough engineer, William Harpur, and opened in 1891. The striking Market House and Guildhall of Penzance (Cornwall) in the area called Green Market, dating to 1837, dominates Market Jew Street. Built of granite, with a giant Ionic portico and topped by a dome, it seems to speak of order and civic pride.

ABOVE OPPOSITE
The Arrival of the Stage Coach at the Sun Inn, Bodmin, Cornwall; *watercolour and pen and black ink over graphite on paper, by Thomas Rowlandson (1756–1827). (Yale Center for British Art, Paul Mellon Collection, USA/The Bridgeman Art Library.)*

The old market building (below) in Penzance (Cornwall) was replaced by the new Market House and Guildhall (below right) built in granite in 1837. The area under the dome was used as a corn exchange.

OLD MARKET, PENZANCE.

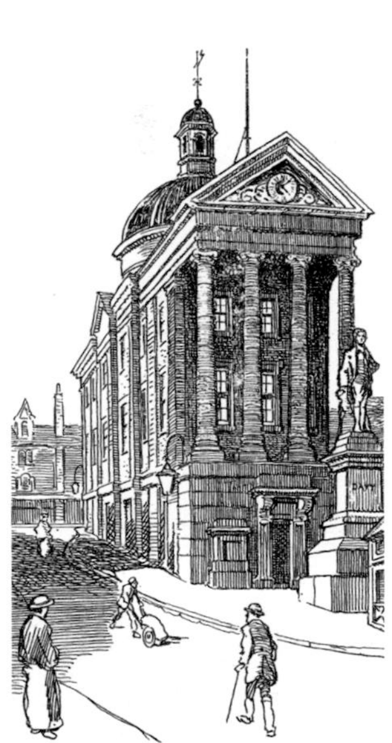

Cirencester: The Shambles *by J. Burden, 1804. Over time, as happened elsewhere, the Market Place was encroached on by permanent buildings. (By kind permission of Gloucestershire Archives Service.)*

In other towns, too, this same spirit led city fathers and private individuals to invest in splendid new developments. It has been said that market halls, often with a mixture of shops and stalls inside,became the working-class equivalent of the middle-class departmental store. In nineteenth-century Newcastle-upon-Tyne the builder and entrepreneur Richard Grainger constructed a large covered market (costing £36,290) at his own expense in the centre of the recently developed area that came to be known as Grainger Town. This took the place of the demolished meat market of 1808. Grainger Market, covering an area between four new streets, was opened in 1835. Inside are a weigh-house and avenues of shops, many of which have been in the same families for generations. The smallest and oldest of these is home to one of the original Marks & Spencer Penny Bazaars, opened in 1895. (The first such stall was started by a Jewish immigrant, Michael Marks, who in 1884 set up a small trestle table in Kirkgate Market, Leeds, selling a wide range of millinery goods and charging the same amount for all items with the slogan: 'Don't ask the price. It's a penny.' His success in business led to a partnership with Tom Spencer and a further development of Penny Bazaars – the forerunners of today's Marks & Spencer stores.) A large vegetable hall, rebuilt after a fire in 1901, is located on the west side of Grainger Market. A picture of this as it looked in 1835 shows produce displayed on the floor as well as on tables.

In the West Midlands the street commissioners of the rapidly expanding town of Birmingham decided to tidy up its open-air market, which for centuries had taken place in the area known as the Bull Ring. This part of the town was cleared and in 1835 a Doric market hall with room for six hundred stalls was opened; towering over the site, it was the largest building in Birmingham. Here flowers, fruit and vegetables, meat and poultry were sold, as well as fancy goods. When in 1851 the new town council took charge of the market, the outgoing street commissioners had a large bronze fountain installed in the middle of the hall to celebrate their achievements. In this hall four thousand people sat down to a dinner of roast beef and plum pudding on Queen Victoria's Coronation Day, 28 June 1838. It was bombed during the Second World War and then swept away as part of a new traffic scheme. Also in the 1830s, Exeter acquired the Lower Market (destroyed in 1942) and the Higher Market (now a shopping mall), with a prize-winning façade that has been described as 'the most magnificent example of a Grecian temple used for a public market', whilst Cirencester took the

Cirencester: Market Place, c. 1840. The infill has been cleared to leave a large open area. (By kind permission of Gloucestershire Archives Office.)

opportunity to clear its marketplace of infill.

In the Wirral Birkenhead received its market hall in 1845, erected by engineers who later would be involved in the construction of the Crystal Palace. Approximately 430 feet long, it has twenty-four bays. The two fountains originally placed in the building have been removed. In Gloucester the Bath-stone Corinthian portico, dating to 1856, is all that is left of the former Eastgate Market. Now fronting a new market, it has stone carvings above its three arches, depicting a cornucopia in the centre, fish on the left and poultry on the right-hand side. There is a flower in the centre of each composite capital topping the giant Corinthian columns. The pediment contains a clock, and the whole structure is surmounted by a bell tower.

Kirkgate Market in Leeds was first opened in 1857, extended in 1875 and reconstructed in 1904.

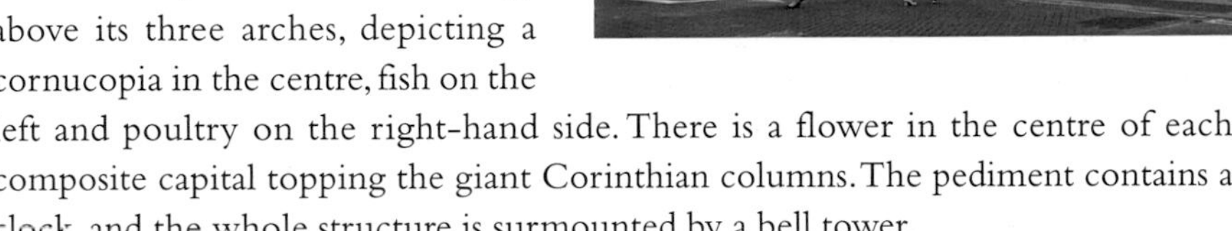

In Edinburgh street vending went on till 1823, when fruit and vegetables moved to a building under the North Bridge, where they remained until 1866, when the Waverley Market was built in Princes Street. However, in Shropshire the market traders of Bridgnorth were not impressed with the new Italianate market hall of 1855. They refused to move in, and the Saturday market has continued underneath and around the seventeenth-century town hall in the High Street into the twenty-first century.

Between 1700 and 1851 (a census year) the population of Leeds increased from 12,000 to 172,000 people, whose daily requirements could not be met by the five privately funded markets dating from the 1820s. As a result, the main thoroughfare, Briggate, was cluttered with large numbers of stalls. So when in 1842 the first elected town council took over from the improvement commissioners, it was decided to allocate £14,000 to a market committee, whose job was to provide the town with a new building. They took their task seriously and made a study of the provisions in Liverpool, Birmingham, Worcester, Birkenhead, Newcastle and Manchester. In 1856 the Leeds Improvement Act prohibited market stalls in Briggate, a rule that was implemented in 1857, when a new market hall, to the design of C. Tilney (the borough surveyor) and Joseph Paxton opened

High Street and town hall, Bridgnorth (Shropshire), where the Saturday market still takes place.

RIGHT
The opening of a new market building was often celebrated by the community. Here flags and bunting decorate Eastbank Market in Southport (Lancashire) on the day it opened in 1879.

to acclaim. A year later the *Leeds Guide* gave the following description: 'The building is of iron and glass, covering an area of 4,040 yards... The style of architecture is Gothic. It has 44 convenient shops on the outside, 35 inside, where there are also four rows of iron stalls. At night this beautiful crystal market hall is well illuminated by 200 gas lights, arranged round handsome cast iron pillars. Altogether it is the most complete structure of its kind in England.'

In addition a large open-air market took place outside the new building on Tuesdays and Saturdays. The rules covering the market included a list of goods that were permitted to be sold and the prohibition of smoking, swearing and the presence of hawkers and dogs. However, space soon ran out and the market was extended in 1875, only to be replaced in 1904. The new building was made of cast iron, steel and glass, and features include twenty-eight clustered Corinthian columns, lantern roofs, a central octagon and dragons supporting a gallery. Today both the indoor and outdoor markets still attract large numbers of customers.

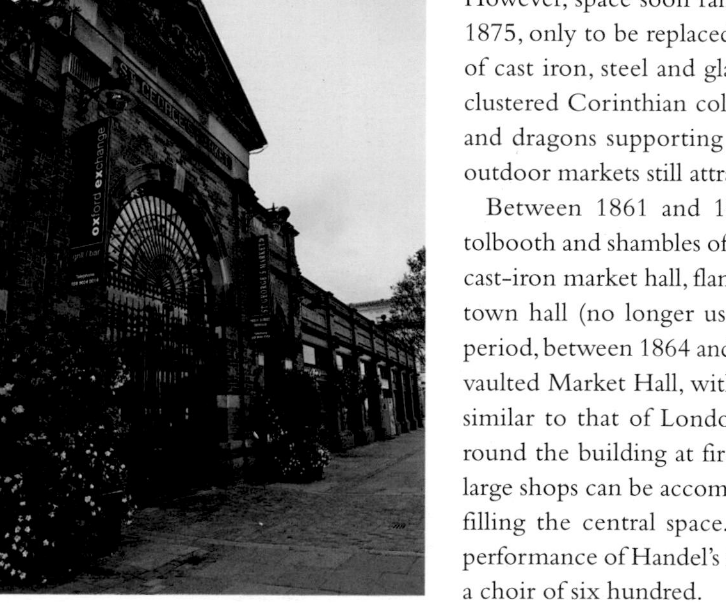

BELOW
St George's Market, Belfast, was built between 1890 and 1896 to the design of the city surveyor.

Between 1861 and 1864 Alfred Waterhouse replaced the tolbooth and shambles of Darlington (Durham) with a glass and cast-iron market hall, flanked by a clock tower at one end and a town hall (no longer used as such) at the other. In the same period, between 1864 and 1866 Derby acquired the vast, tunnel-vaulted Market Hall, with a roof that was constructed in a way similar to that of London's St Pancras station. A gallery runs round the building at first-floor level, underneath which forty large shops can be accommodated. Added to this were 150 stalls filling the central space. The opening was celebrated with a performance of Handel's *Messiah,* involving an organ, a band and a choir of six hundred.

Of the dozen or so covered markets that could once be found in Belfast, Northern Ireland, only St George's Market still remains. Replacing an open market, it was built in brick with sandstone dressings by the city surveyor between 1890 and 1896 and has a top-lit roof resting on cast-iron pillars. One side is lined with shops and inside are 248 stalls. Above the classical-style arches are Latin and Irish inscriptions, which in translation say: 'What shall we give in return for so much?' and 'Red hand of Ireland'. Above the main entrance is the Belfast coat of arms.

Setting off for Market, *oil on board, by Edward Bird (1772–1819). (By kind permission of the Wolverhampton Art Gallery)*

In Devon and Cornwall markets are often called 'pannier markets' on account of the large baskets, or panniers, in which farmers' wives would bring their produce. They might ride to town along well-worn cross-country routes, leaning their baskets against the pack-saddles that kept the panniers in place, or accompany their husbands going to market on their own business. (An example of a pack-saddle can be viewed in the Elizabethan House Museum in Totnes [Devon].) In his book *In Search of England* (first published in 1927) H.V. Morton describes the scene of the weekly proceedings as witnessed by him in Barnstaple (Devon):'The body of the cart is occupied by Sarah's brown calf under a net or by three protesting piglets. Beside the farmer's wife are two big wicker-work baskets, known by the old name "panniers". They are covered with butter muslin. In one basket are the biggest, reddest, and shiniest strawberries you ever saw in your life, a great jug of brown Devonshire cream, several pounds of bright gold butter, and a cheese; in the other lie two dead fowls and a duck, trussed and plucked, their intimate internals neatly pinned to their wings.' Having arrived at their destination, the couple split up:'The wife arms her panniers and goes off in one direction; the farmer ... makes off with the calf or the piglets in another. Husband and wife will not meet again till the end of the day, and then they will jog home together in an empty cart, talking finance.'

Early nineteenth-century pack-saddle on display in the Elizabethan House Museum, Totnes (Devon).

Generally pannier markets had no fixed stalls or shops (though in a later period some might be added), only benches and trestle tables called 'sittings' on which farmers' wives could display their baskets. A yearly rent, as well as a market-day toll, had to be paid for the use of the sitting. An early example of a pannier market was built in

Honiton (Devon) by the Paving Trust Commissioners *c.* 1823. Now a shop, the ground floor was lined with stalls selling farm produce, whilst the first floor was used as an assembly room. The custom of throwing hot pennies from the balcony into the crowds during the opening of the annual charter fair in July is still maintained here. In Dartmouth (Devon) the pannier market was built in 1828–9 on the site of a drained mill pool. Single-storey lock-up units and an open, though roofed, area for booths surround a central two-storey building, which originally was open at ground level. The backs of the stalls enclosing the courtyard form a wall with gates, which are locked when the market is closed. As mentioned before, the walls are covered with boards detailing the tolls charged for the various products offered for sale, including 'One Penny for every Basket, or Parcel, of Carrots, Parsnips, or Turnips, not exceeding one Bushel' and 'One Penny for any Quantity of Cabbage Plants, not exceeding Five Hundred'.

The Pannier Market, Barnstaple (Devon), was built in 1855 as a result of public pressure after a cholera outbreak. Originally it was called the Vegetable Market.

The restored Pannier Market in Tiverton (Devon) is hidden from the main street in the centre of the town. Built in 1830 on a former bowling green and much altered in 1876, it is lit from above to make it easy for customers inspecting the articles for sale. The clock cupola adds interest to the building, which on one side is faced by a row of single-storeyed booths offering further commercial opportunities. On a smaller scale, the Pannier Market at Launceston (Cornwall) was erected in 1840. The building is of particular interest because of its curved roof slating. Great Torrington (Devon) acquired its shopping amenity in 1842. Constructed by a local builder, it features a corridor lined with retail units behind a classical façade. The Pannier Market in Barnstaple (Devon), dating to 1855, came about as the result of public pressure after a cholera outbreak. It was built on a rather grand scale behind the Guildhall and, as already mentioned, nine years later had the Corn Exchange, now a theatre, added to it. Consisting of a glass and timber roof resting on iron columns, it was originally called the Vegetable Market. Here, as described by H.V. Morton, 'about 500 farmers' wives and daughters [sat] before their stalls on which they display[ed] their week's work' for it was 'generally speaking, a woman's market. For every farmer who [had] a stall there [were] at least fifty women.'

In 1859 the Duke of Bedford decided to improve the town centre of Tavistock (Devon) on a grand scale. A substantial area was cleared to accommodate a new guildhall, town hall and pannier market – the last approached via the first or through a pair of splendid cast-iron gates. The local granite used for the floor and arches makes for a rather sombre interior. In the same county, Bideford paid £4,200 for its pannier market, which was constructed in 1853–4 and included a fish market, butchery stalls and a corn exchange. After the opening ceremony nearly two hundred people sat down to a public dinner, followed by a promenade concert. The pannier market built *c.* 1960 in Plymouth as part of the post-war reconstruction of the city centre is wholly functional under its concrete roof.

Up to this period livestock had usually been sold in the marketplace, where farmers shared the area with traders of foodstuffs and other goods, though sometimes a separate marketplace might be available, as was the case in King's Lynn (Norfolk) and Wetherby (Yorkshire). As we have seen already, nearby streets also might be used, as happened in Leeds, where the cattle market was held in Vicar Lane, the horse fair in Upper Headrow and the pig market in Lower Headrow. In Market Harborough (Leicestershire) the town square was used as a livestock market until 1903. In Tetbury (Gloucestershire) animals were sold along Gumstool Hill, with sheep and cattle occupying opposite sides of the road until they were moved to the open space of The Chipping, there to be joined by market stalls selling a variety of goods. As in so many towns, in Colchester and Chelmsford (both in Essex) and Thornbury (Gloucestershire) the cattle market took place in the High Street. In Honiton (Devon) cattle and sheep were sold at one end of the High Street and horses at the other end, with the general market (which still exists) in between. In Shaftesbury (Dorset) sheep were tethered on Gold Hill, and in Castle Cary (Somerset) the livestock market was held on Bailey Hill, behind the Market House, where in 1777 the Round House or lock-up was built to deal with those who created a nuisance. Until the end of the nineteenth century, in Bromyard (Herefordshire), too, the livestock market was held in the street, and the High Street from the Falcon to the top of the town was known as the 'Beast Market'.

Waltham Abbey (Essex) sheep market c. 1906. *(By kind permission of John Hannavy.)*

In all cases sheep pens and the posts to which cattle were tied were set up weekly, bringing complaints about obstruction of the public highway, the noise, and the mess left behind at the end of the day. In Stafford there were complaints about 'disgusting filth' and the animals bringing 'terror and alarm to young ladies'. Outside the town hall of Skipton (Yorkshire) a flagstone path leading to the church can be observed, cutting across the cobblestones. This was laid to help the vicar make his way from the vicarage to the church without getting his robes dirtied with the muck created by the cattle market. There was also the hazard of panic-stricken beasts breaking loose, a not uncommon occurrence, causing havoc, if not injury. Shopkeepers and residents often kept their doors shut in fear of a bolting animal charging in. Such an event took place in early twentieth-century Morpeth (Northumberland) when William Moore walked a cow from the station through the main street to the Newmarket and the creature decided to enter a house, where it calmly walked up the stairs and entered a bedroom. In Chichester (Sussex) each market day sheep pens were erected between the Cross and Little London, with iron posts provided nearby so that farmers could tie up their horses. As elsewhere, during the rest of the week the empty postholes left behind when the market equipment had been removed posed a hazard.

To improve on this situation, throughout the nineteenth and into the early twentieth century local authorities started to provide separate, usually enclosed areas away, though not far, from town centres. Here, behind a wall or metal paling, sometimes with ornamental gates, livestock markets were developed containing permanent pens and posts. In St Ives (Cambridgeshire) the two entrance lodges of

Bedford Pig Market, *by William Henry Pyne (1769–1843). (Cecil Higgins Art Gallery, Bedford, / The Bridgeman Art Library.)*

the former cattle market, opened in 1886, still exist, enhanced, like the railings, with the town's crest of four bulls' heads, and bearing the motto S*udere non sopore* ('By work, not by sleep' – a pun on 'Slepe', the former name of the town). The area was turned into a bus station in the 1970s. Within the grounds, a market office might be built, such as the Settling Rooms in Market Harborough (Leicestershire), dating to 1903, the nineteenth-century counting house of Bromsgrove (Worcestershire), now in the nearby Avoncroft Museum of Buildings, or the market building in Tring (Hertfordshire) (which in 2008 was in the process of being turned into a local history museum), where farmers did their bargaining and completed their business deals. Totnes (Devon) still has its ticket office in a street called 'The Lamb'. From 1845, when a tax imposed on auctions was abolished, auction rings became important fixtures and can be found in most working livestock markets. Here, often summoned by a bell, farmers would gather – as they still do, to bid for animals, usually cattle or horses, shown individually as they are made to walk round the ring. Normally sheep were and are sold in multiples, standing in their pens as auctioneers point them out to interested farmers and butchers. A further development was the introduction of the weigh-house, where animals are put on scales before they enter the ring or pens. In this way buyers are provided with accurate information, where before they had to guess, though long experience meant they were never far out in their estimation of the weight of an animal.

In Leeds a new livestock market was developed by the Leeds Improvement Commission on a plot of ground bordering Kirkgate and Vicar Lane, so that in August 1822 the *Leeds Intelligencer* could state: 'measures are now in progress for removing the cow and pig markets into the Vicar's Croft; where also the country dealers, with vegetables and fruit, who supply our hucksters with these articles, will have to take their carts; a portion of the Croft being appropriated for their reception. This will materially relieve the pressure in Briggate [the town's main thoroughfare] on a market day.' Animals, fruit and vegetables were sold on Tuesdays and Saturdays, and hay, straw and teasels (used in the woollen industry) every day of the week. Those coming from a distance could leave their carts and produce in the market on the evenings before market days. At first the market was unpaved, but later an area of 8,000 square yards was covered with best-quality stone. When the site was needed for an extended covered market, the animals were moved to an area in town called the 'Smithfield Cattle Market', a name derived from the famous market in London and commonly used for areas where livestock was sold, and often also with the pubs associated with them. Land bought by Manchester Corporation near Shudehill in 1846 was developed for a number of market activities, including livestock sales and a covered market, which by 1900 was the largest in Britain. In Melton Mowbray (Leicestershire) animals had been sold by the Sheep Cross in Nottingham Street for centuries. Here as many as 60,000 sheep might be sold in a year and there

The entrance lodges of the former cattle market in St Ives (Cambridgeshire), built in 1886.

A cattle sale at Reading (Berkshire) with Mr L. T. Phillips leading a dairy shorthorn cow round the ring. (By kind permission of the Museum of English Rural Life, Reading University.)

were constant complaints by the townspeople, who wanted to see the area cleaned up. As a result a new cattle market was built on the outskirts of the town in 1870, where a modern version can still be found: a busy centre for the sales of cattle, sheep and horses, and fur and feather auctions (which include hamsters, songbirds, chickens, ducks and other pets and small animals), farmers' markets and antiques markets. In Bath (Somerset) the Beast Market was moved to Walcott Street and in Oxford the bus station in Gloucester Green marks the site of the former cattle market. (Here, the former Welsh Pony pub in George Street was a reminder of the Welsh drovers walking the animals into town to be sold.) Though in 1827 the council of Stranraer (Dumfries and Galloway) agreed to a petition to have the sale of cattle, horses and swine banned from the streets, it took some years before an alternative site, near the harbour, was found. At the same time a weighing machine for the use of traders and farmers was provided nearby. Towards the end of the nineteenth century Winslow (Buckinghamshire) developed a cattle market not far from the marketplace. Here pens, a disused cattle ring and a weigh-house were still in evidence when the last sheep were sold early in 2008, as the market moved to more up-to-date premises elsewhere. Also in the late Victorian period the Rothschild family provided a cattle market in Tring (Hertfordshire), taking the animals away from the High Street into new premises in Brook Street. In Halstead (Essex) the livestock element of the market on Market Hill was moved to a separate sale yard.

Though most animals walked to market, some were taken on barges along the waterways. In this way Oxfordshire farmers would convey their animals down the Thames to London. With the introduction of the railways, many livestock markets were moved to be close to the station, allowing animals to be loaded off and on trains without the stress of having to walk to and from their destination. In Atherstone (Warwickshire) a passage was constructed underneath the railway line as it was being laid, so that the animals that had been sold in the nearby market did not have to use the level crossing. Early on, stations started to provide cattle docks or pens along the platform. Animals would be herded into these as they left or before boarding a train. Remains of these pens can be found along the Severn Valley Railway in Shropshire, where a restored specimen can be seen at Highley station. In Tetbury (Gloucestershire) the livestock market moved from The Chipping to the bottom of Gumstool Hill in 1889 with the arrival of the railway. Here two auctioneers' huts and a few sheep pens have been restored as a permanent reminder. Near the derelict station are further, rather overgrown pens, left in 1964 when the line was closed. In Machynllyth (Powys) livestock was taken away from the main market area in Maengwyn Street to a yard nearer the station, where till 1932 the last of the traditional Welsh *porthmyn* (drovers), Dafydd Isaac and John George from Ceredigion, brought their sheep. Often paddocks were provided as holding areas. In Downham Market (Norfolk) cattle brought for sale were put on the Town Green near Railway Road, where iron gates were used to prevent the animals from wandering off. In many towns the pubs were allowed extended opening hours on market days and notice of this could be found on the buildings, as can be observed in Kirkby Lonsdale (Cumbria) and Corwen (Denbighshire).

Statistics for the movement of animals in England and Wales, quoted in *The British Almanac* for 1864, mention 226,439 horses, 2,123,833 cattle, 6,076,908 sheep and 1,270,561 pigs. After the Second World War road transport started to compete with the railways and gradually took over, particularly after the closure of many rural lines following the Beeching Report of 1963. This in turn led to the development of larger, out-of-town sites, and towards the end of the twentieth century many livestock markets were closed to make way for housing, shops and supermarkets and car parks – a process that is still continuing. Reasons for this include the need for town renewal, epidemic outbreaks of swine fever or foot and mouth disease, and sometimes lack of the money needed to update premises to modern standards. Westerham (Kent), Ludlow and Oswestry (both in Shropshire), Thornbury (Gloucestershire), Dorchester (Dorset),

Produce ready for sale in Worcester market in 1949. (By kind permission of the Museum of English Rural Life, Reading University.)

ABOVE *The cattle market in Tring (Hertfordshire), built by the Rothschild family at the beginning of the twentieth century, helped to remove animals from the High Street, where a livestock market had been held since the thirteenth century. (By kind permission of Mike Bass.)*

Bromsgrove (Worcestershire), Lichfield (Staffordshire), Beverley (Yorkshire) and Lewes (Sussex) have all lost their cattle markets. In Cirencester (Gloucestershire) Lord and Lady Apsley had the market's office building, including its stone bearing the Bathurst coronet and entwined Bs, carefully taken down for re-erection elsewhere, before a leisure centre was constructed on the former market site. At Slough (Berkshire) the cattle market in William Street (now the university car park), established there in the mid nineteenth century to be near the station, was moved to Wexham Street in the 1970s to allow the local authorities to redevelop the site. Soon turnover started to diminish and after an outbreak of swine fever it closed in 1988, the site being used for housing. In 1985 Morpeth (Northumberland) for the first time in eight hundred years no longer sold livestock in the market, where one auctioneer, George Strachan, remembered that 'The buyers who came to the auction always stood in exactly the same position round the auction ring and bought the same stock every week'. Because of a charter of 1597 decreeing that the market must be held within the city boundaries, Hereford needed an Act of Parliament (passed in 2007) before it could start implementing its plans for relocation.

FARLEFT
Notice on the Royal Hotel, Kirkby Lonsdale (Cumbria), relating to extended opening hours on market days.

LEFT
The end of the line – the overgrown railway cattle dock in the derelict station yard at Tetbury (Gloucestershire).

However, not all markets have moved away. In Castle Douglas (Dumfries and Galloway) the Auction Marts – the primary market for the Galloway breed of cattle in Britain – can be found in the town. When the market authorities of Bakewell (Derbyshire) decided that the ancient marketplace was no longer adequate, they built state-of-the-art new premises in a building designed acoustically to help reduce the noise of the livestock inside. Part of the Agricultural Business Centre, it is only a short walk away from the heart of the town. Here, as in the many other markets of Britain, auctions go on in the time-honoured way, but assisted by modern technology. Amongst other things, farmers can have auction market reports sent straight to their mobile phones.

OPPOSITE BOTTOM
Livestock driven into the centre of Modbury (Devon) caused severe problems for traffic along this major route to Plymouth. In 1934 it was reported that the cattle market 'after being in existence for 600 years' was 'in danger of being closed'. (By kind permission of the Museum of English Rural Life, Reading University.)

BELOW
Newark livestock market, Nottinghamshire.

Chapter Six

LONDON

THOUGH vastly superior in size to any other city in the British Isles, London's first and foremost role has been that of a market town, in the widest sense possible. Buying and selling in all their permutations have been its lifeblood. Though, unlike most market towns, this vast metropolis was never incorporated, it did receive rights from Edward the Confessor, later confirmed by William the Conqueror, which allowed it to look after its own affairs, including matters relating to markets. After all, to keep the city prosperous and growing, its population had to have regular access to food supplies that were wholesome and affordable to most people. Over the centuries various monarchs granted the city charters designed to protect its trade; for example, a market charter of 1327 stated that no market should set up within 7 miles of London, except at Southwark and Westminster.

The Roman author Tacitus, writing in about AD 67, says that when his countrymen arrived here in the years between AD 43 and 60 they found a thriving trading community. However, it is generally believed, in spite of evidence of prehistoric activity, that the first real settlers were the Romans, who gave the place the name Londinium. The wooden bridge they built across the River Thames, on a site very close to the present London Bridge, helped the development not only of what later came to be known as 'the City', to the north, but also the very important suburb of Southwark, on the south bank.

The city was built on and between two hills, one now the site of St Paul's Cathedral, the other Cornhill, on either side of the Walbrook stream (today hidden in a culvert). Inside its protective wall, following the standard Roman town-planning pattern, a large, square forum, or marketplace, with its temple and basilica (town hall and courts), took up an important position as the centre of administrative and trading activities. It was situated close to present-day Leadenhall and Gracechurch Street. The first Saxons to arrive, shunning city life as they did elsewhere, settled to the west of the Roman town, along the Strand (close to today's Aldwych), calling the place Lundenwic, *wic* meaning 'market town'. This became part of an important trading network of Saxon settlements in northern Europe and may have been the 'metropolis' mentioned by the Venerable Bede in *c.* 730: 'a mart of many peoples coming by land and sea'. However, after severe Viking raids, starting at the end of the eighth century, the Saxons sought shelter within the Roman walls, and the city of London re-established itself on the earlier site. On the south side of the river the 'great cheaping [i.e. market] town called Southwarke', so described in the Norwegian Olaf Sagas, was also thriving.

On the north bank of the Thames two important landing, and therefore trading, centres were established along the waterfront, at Billingsgate and at Queenhithe. Inland two open markets for food appeared, one on either side of the Walbrook: Westcheap (later Cheapside), the larger of the two, occupying the widest street of the

OPPOSITE
Drover Road, Croydon, Market Day; *oil on canvas, by John Burell Read (died 1904). (Croydon Art Collection, Museum of Croydon/The Bridgeman Art Library.)*

City, and Eastcheap. In Westcheap the rule was that booths were to stand in the middle of the street, between the gutters, so that carts and pedestrians could pass them on both sides. At night traders might sleep under their collapsible stalls. Various market routes, used by both traders and their customers, developed, amongst them the present Gray's Inn Road and Tottenham Court Road. Bread Street provided a direct route from Queenhithe to Cheapside. Drovers brought their animals down Liverpool Road, Goswell Road and Aldersgate Street after a period of rest in the cattle lairs of Islington. Equally, the routes along St John Street and Farringdon Lane, Turnmill Street and Cowcross Street in Clerkenwell were used by traders and drovers on their way to Smithfield and the cattle market at Cowcross next to it.

Though potentially traders could set up anywhere in town, certain areas soon came to be associated with the sales of a particular type of produce. At the end of the twelfth century William Fitzstephen, clerk to Thomas Becket, in his short description of the capital (written in Latin) stated: 'the vendors of the various commodities … have each their separate stations which they take every morning'. Street names such as Milk Street, Bread Street, Honey Lane, Poultry, Wood Street and Ironmonger Lane, all still to be found, give an indication of what was sold there in the past. Panyer Alley may be named after basket or pannier makers producing containers for the nearby bakers. (A stone relief of a boy sitting on such a basket – the Panyer Boy – is set into the wall of the corner building near Newgate Street.)

Generally markets were for country people ('foreigners', or outsiders) selling their produce, whilst London citizens had shops. The early markets were held on trestle tables, or 'boordes', in the street, open to the elements. However, soon 'improvements' were made, in the way we have already observed in other towns, where open market areas experienced an infill of more permanent structures. In his book *The Survey of London*, published in 1598, the historian John Stow gives an interesting description

Escheape: Market *from Hugh Alley's* A Caveatt for the Citty of London OR a forewarninge of offences against penall lawes, *dated 1598. Note the butchers' displays of meat in front of the buildings on the opposite side of the street. (By kind permission of the Folger Shakespeare Library.)*

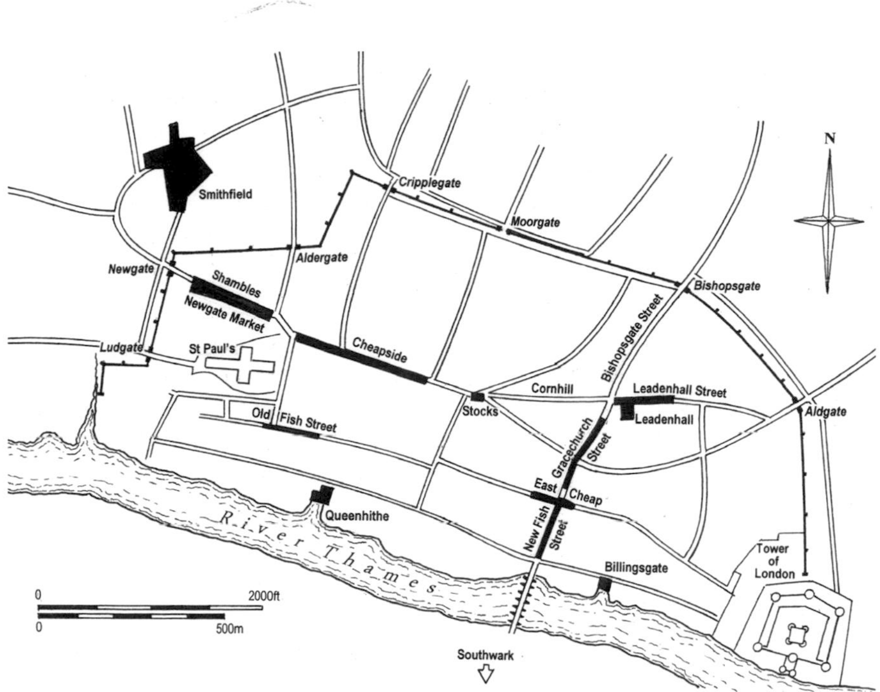

Map of the main medieval market sites in London before the Great Fire of 1666.

of the evolution of temporary market stalls into more solid buildings: 'stallboards were of old time set up by the butchers to show and sell their flesh meat upon, over the which stallboards they first built sheds to keep off the weather, but since that, encroaching by little and little, they have made their stallboards and sheds fair houses...' The fishmongers were equally guilty. We are told that in 'Old Fish Street is one row of small houses, placed along in the middle of Knightriders Streete... These houses, now possessed by fishmongers, were at the first but moveable boards [or stalls], set out on market days, to show their fish there to be sold; but procuring licence to set up sheds, they grew to shops, and by little and little to tall houses, of three or four stories in height.'

The meat trade was particularly well represented in the city. From the twelfth century butchers had their stalls in Bridge Street (now Fish Street Hill), Eastcheap and at the Shambles. The last, situated in a continuation of Cheapside, towards Newgate, was already mentioned in 1196, when St Nicholas's Church was built next to an abattoir and came to be known as 'St Nicholas by the Shambles'. Here two rows of butchers' stalls stood back to back in the middle of the road, forming Middle Row.

At least from the reign of Edward III the butcher's trade had been recognised as causing health hazards. Though there were slaughterhouses in Eastcheap, elsewhere animals were killed in the streets, causing traffic obstruction and the pollution of blood and offal left in the gutters. Pudding Lane (now mostly remembered as the site where the Great Fire of London started in 1666) is named after butchers' offal, or 'puddings'. John Stow wrote of 'Rother lane, or Red Rose lane ... now commonly called Pudding lane, because the butchers of Eastcheap have their scalding house for hogs there, and their puddings, with other filth of beasts, are voided down that way to their dung boats on the Thames'. The Butchers' Company had to make sure that

The panyer boy*, a stone relief of 1688, can be found in Panyer Alley, EC4. It is thought to refer to the presence of the makers of panniers for the bakers of Bread Street.*

all offal and other rubbish produced by the trade were disposed of in a responsible way. There is a reminder of this in the traditional presentation of a boar's head to every new Lord Mayor at the Mansion House – payment for the use of a piece of land 'for cleaning the entrails of beasts'. As we have seen in other towns, people regularly asked to have the butchers' shambles removed, but without success. In 1593 Simon Kellawaye, amongst others, advised on the importance of clean water in the fight against disease, in particular water free from animal waste.

Already in 1274, in an effort to improve the situation by the removal of the butchers' and fishmongers' stalls from Cheapside, the Lord Mayor, Henry le Walys, erected a building called the 'Stocks Market' or 'Les Stokkes'. (Some say it was named after the only pair of fixed stocks in the city, which were situated in front of it; others that the words refer to the stalls or booths used by the traders.) This was permitted under a charter given by Edward I, which allowed a market to be built next to St Mary Woolchurch. It stood very close to a crossing over the Walbrook, on the site of the present Mansion House, and had stalls inside and out. It was leased to a number of fishmongers, who were ordered to sublet to members of their own profession, as well as to butchers. Late sixteenth-century drawings show the former displaying their wares on trestle tables or 'boordes', whilst the latter suspended the animal carcasses from railings. The Stocks Market was rebuilt several times and in 1645 was described as a 'great stonehouse', with the butchers' stalls to the north and fish slabs to the south. The rent paid for these went towards the upkeep of London Bridge. In 1543, when there were twenty-five 'boordes' for fishmongers and eighteen butchers' stalls, that amounted to £82 3s.

Fishmongers, who were of particular importance in Lent and the many other periods of fasting, could also be found elsewhere in the city. In 1321 it was ruled that, apart from the Stocks Market, fish could be sold only in Bridge Street and Old Fish Street, where, as we have seen in John Stow's description, a row of fishmongers' shops had developed from moveable stalls, occupying the centre of the road. Here fresh fish from nearby Queenhithe was brought daily. Freshwater fish, brought in from the country, could be purchased by St Margaret's Church in Bridge Street, by St Mary Magdalen's Church in Old Fish Street and by the conduit in Cheapside.

Fruit, herbs, roots and other victuals came in via the river, to be landed at Billingsgate and, after 1566, also at Queenhithe. Produce, including cheese, butter and poultry, was also brought in overland by country traders, who were restricted to dealing between certain hours, on allocated days of the week, which differed between markets and might change over time. Stalls selling fruit, vegetables and dairy produce could be found in Newgate Market (where in 1377 cheese and butter were confined to the area between St Nicholas Shambles and Newgate), Cheapside, Gracechurch Market, the open-air street market at Leadenhall and Southwark. Just as the butchers were admonished for the pollution they caused, so too were the fruit and vegetable sellers. In 1588 those in Cheapside were told not to clean their produce in the street, 'for we find by experience that that leads to great annoyance and hath byn some cause of infection'. The peascod sellers were ordered to sweep up their shells regularly. An Act of 1628 ordered that in Westminster market 'stalls of all fishmongers and sellers of hearbes, rootes or any other things' and any 'trash in the street that might stopp or hinder the passage' should be cleared away.

Throughout the centuries the city authorities kept a strict eye on the availability and price of corn, anxious to ensure that the population would not starve – or riot when hunger overwhelmed it. For this reason they would step in when prices became too high because of a shortage, maybe as the result of a bad harvest, and buy in stocks in order to sell at a reasonable level. There were occasional corn markets in the churchyard of St Michael at Corn in Paternoster Row, first mentioned in 1181, and also grain markets at Queenhithe, Billingsgate, Cornhill, Fenchurch Street (it is thought that nearby Seething Lane received its name, derived from the Old English for 'full of chaff', because of its proximity to the corn market here), Gracechurch Street, and at Newgate Pavement, from where in 1445 it moved to a purpose-built grain store in Leadenhall Market.

Leadenhall takes its name from a private mansion with a lead roof, belonging to the Neville family. In 1345 it was designated as the place where 'foreign' or non-citizen traders could sell poultry (only citizen poulterers were allowed to trade in the street called Poultry), though later the rules were changed. In 1411 the estate was sold to the City Corporation and the house was rebuilt as a granary so that corn could be stored, making the city more self-sufficient with regards to this very important staple food. In 1445 the site was turned into a general market for grain and dairy products, later adding leather and wool, nails and lead. It was an important market for poultry, and geese, capons, hens, rabbits (one source mentions 'runners' and 'suckers'), river mallard, teal, larks, snipe, woodcock, partridge, pheasant, swans, cranes, bustards, herons, shovellers, bitterns, storks, plovers, quail and curlews were sold here.

London's livestock market was at Smithfield (originally 'Smoothfield', described as a 'plain grassy space just outside the city walls'). It covered about 3 acres. In 1173 William Fitzstephen wrote: 'There is, without one of the gates, immediately in the suburb, a certain smooth field in name and in reality. There every Friday, unless it be one of the more solemn festivals, is a noted show of well-bred horses exposed for sale. The earls, barons and knights, who are at the time resident in the city, as well as most of the citizens, flock thither either to look on or buy … in one part are horses better adapted to esquires…' Some years later, in 1305, oxen were sold for 5s. 6d each. Cattle, sheep and pigs were allocated different areas within the market and, as elsewhere in the city, a distinction was made between local and 'foreign' dealers. In 1379 cattle belonging to Londoners were given an area near Aldersgate, whilst those selling pigs were told to occupy a spot near St Bartholomew's Hospital. 'Foreign' traders could use the areas between these sites. By the mid sixteenth century permanent sheep pens were in place, which by 1568 were let at 6d each on market days – Wednesdays and Fridays. All sales of horses were to happen in the open marketplace so that there were witnesses to the deal – a rule we have seen observed elsewhere. Dealers from outside the city could not buy from others in that position except on Wednesdays and Fridays between 11 a.m. and 1 p.m.

In Southwark, on the other side of the river, a thriving medieval market had established itself outside St Thomas's Hospital. This eventually spilled over on to the southern side of London Bridge and in 1276 was declared a public nuisance for causing a traffic obstruction. In the fifteenth century this market was overtaken by a new one in the High Street, which in 1550 was allowed to operate on Mondays, Wednesdays, Fridays and Saturdays. Here in 1548 traders of fish, poultry, herbs, fruit and bread were allocated 'standings'.

There were many rules covering market operations, all described in *The Laws of the Market*, published by the City authorities. Many of these were meant to protect the consumer from high prices and fraud. To make sure that all dealings were above board (literally), there were set times and places that people had to adhere to. Some rules were there to protect city traders against competition from outside traders. As we have already seen, dealers from elsewhere were given areas to trade in separate from those allocated to citizens; for example, at the end of the sixteenth century 'foreign' poulterers had trading places outside Grey Friars monastery in Newgate Street and at the crossroads of Cornhill, Leadenhall Street, Gracechurch Street and Bishopsgate, whilst London poulterers stood in front of St Nicholas Shambles and by St Michael Cornhill. In 1521 there were complaints about London traders sending their servants, dressed as countrymen, to areas reserved for non-residents, in order to increase their profits at the expense of the 'foreign' traders. Another rule stated that only citizens could trade with non-citizen as well as citizen dealers. Non-citizens could not trade with one another, except after a certain time in the day, as we have seen in Smithfield. All this was to the benefit of the London traders, of course.

Trading times were strictly enforced. Some markets were open from dawn to dusk, others closed at midday. In 1378 butchers were told to close 'before the time for candles being lighted' (it is easier to cheat in semi-darkness than in the daylight). In Cheapside a bell was rung an hour before the curfew bell, to indicate that trading should stop. At Southwark a bailiff rang the bell at 2 p.m. in the winter and at 3 p.m. in the summer. 'Evechepynges' (markets held in the evenings, usually on feast days) were obliged to close when the bell was rung half an hour after sunset. Whilst at first meat, though no other produce, was sold on Sundays until 10 a.m., from 1442 trading of any kind on the sabbath was forbidden to all.

Selling outside market areas was frowned on and over time boundaries were fixed. In 1364 this happened with the two areas along the riverfront where fish was brought ashore. In 1379 the exact limits of Smithfield were laid down, and in 1414 those of East Street and Old Market Street.

As we have already seen, in addition to the many local rules enacted by town and city officials nationwide, there were also the universal ones covering forestalling, regrating and engrossing. These were meant to stop middlemen making what was considered an unfair, because unearned, profit as they did not add to the value of the products for sale but by dealing in them put up their price. The prohibition was intended to promote fair trading, at customary prices, which should remain constant. In London the fishmongers seemed to contravene these rules regularly. John Stow mentions that in the eighteenth year of the reign of Edward I both the 'Stock-fishmongers and Salt-fishmongers ... were, for forestalling, etc., contrary to the laws and constitutions of the city, fined to the king at five hundred marks...' A late sixteenth-century complaint mentions 'certain heringe whiche were forstalled and engroced by divers women'. And in June 1600 Thomas Atkins, fishmonger, was fined 20s for forestalling two hundred codfish before they came to market. A further rule stated that traders had to accept if the set price was offered, and they were not allowed to take unsold goods back home in order to sell them somewhere else on another day.

In order to keep staple foods at a reasonable and fair price, the authorities set the price for bread and other basic commodities via the assizes (a statute allowing them to settle the weight, measure or price of a product), taking into account the cost of raw materials. Regular inspections were part of a strict control over quality, weight and measure. On taking office, a new Lord Mayor would take an oath promising to keep a close eye on the assize of bread, ale, fish, corn, flesh and other victuals, also to make sure that the correct weights and measures were used, a standard set of which was kept at the Guildhall (just as we have seen in other towns).

There were many different measures for corn, salt, coals and fruit. A royal proclamation of 1587 commanded officers of market towns to obtain copies of the recently established standard weights from the Exchequer, to test their own weights by, which would be stamped if found in order. These in turn could then be used to check traders' weights and measures. In May 1600 the Keeper of the Guildhall was told to bring the city's bushel, gallon and pint to Vincent Skinner for trial at the Exchequer. Anyone found with unstamped or faulty weights had them removed by two members of the Founders' Company, for recasting by the Keeper of the Guildhall. By the mid 1590s the authorities had provided scales in all the markets and the Clerk of the Market was required to check these regularly. In addition there were other official inspectors, including three meal weighers, as well as private informers and members of the various livery companies checking for irregularities. John Stow mentions that some of these inspectors ordered alehouse keepers found with faulty measures to send a quantity of the liquid to the hospitals. At other times the failed objects would be publicly burned in Cheapside.

As elsewhere, punishments might include being put in the stocks or pillory. In 1319 William Sperlynge 'of West Hamme' was pilloried for trying to sell rotten meat, which was burned under his nose, whilst in 1372 Margery Hove, described as a 'fisshwyfe', was put in the thew (pillory for women) for selling rotten fish, which was also burnt in front of her.

Towards the end of the sixteenth century it was found that many of the rules were being broken. The Book of Fines shows numerous cases of people forestalling, engrossing and regrating, partly because with a growing population it was impossible for everyone growing food to come to market regularly and so middlemen were needed. Even so, as already mentioned, the statute regarding these rules was not abolished until 1772 and in the early eighteenth century Daniel Defoe mentions 'the liberty taken by the butchers, to go up to Islington, and to Whitechapel, and buy of the country drovers, who bring cattle to town; but this is called forestalling the market, and is not allowed by law'.

In the thriving town, space was at a premium and traders were regularly found in areas not allocated to their trade or to their status as citizen or non-citizen. Some traders took up more than their fair share of space and had to be restricted – in 1588 root sellers were told to bring no more than three baskets. Trading times were not always kept to, with markets staying open beyond the statutory hours and Sunday dealing taking place in certain markets, including butchers killing and dressing animals in preparation for the market on Monday. The nave of St Paul's Cathedral was used by vendors, with horses and mules being led through the building, a return to medieval ways long since forbidden.

By the end of the sixteenth century three market houses had been built: one at Newgate, described by Stow as possessing 'A fair, new, and strong frame of timber, covered with lead', one (with a bell turret) at Southwark, and one at Queenhithe. All three were enlarged some years later, to accommodate growing trade.

As the population grew, with an increasing number of people drawn to the thriving city, London started to expand beyond its original boundaries, particularly westwards. By the beginning of the seventeenth century the City and that other important settlement along the River Thames, Westminster, had, as Celia Fiennes would have it a century later, 'so joyned it makes up but one vast building with all the subburbbs'. After the Reformation, with the dissolution of the monasteries, former church-owned sites had become available for wealthy people to acquire and develop. The resulting newly occupied areas needed their own markets and these now came to be provided by individuals as private investment. For this a charter had to be obtained from the king, who, as elsewhere, often asked for a substantial payment. The Reformation had brought a change in attitude from medieval paternalism, with its many restrictive rules aimed at fairness, to a more individualistic approach that looked for private profit.

Outside the city walls the Earls (later Dukes) of Bedford started to develop the site of a garden that had belonged to Westminster Abbey and had been granted to them in 1552. Here at Covent Garden a small market existed that had begun with the sales of surplus produce from their fruit and vegetable plots by both the abbey monks and a few people from the nearby countryside. This market continued, with stalls arranged against the garden wall of the newly built Bedford House, and this did not change when in the first half of the seventeenth century Inigo Jones was appointed to create a splendid new square, in the classical style, attracting the most fashionable people as residents. A shortage of money (the king had demanded £2,000 for the licence to develop) meant that only two sides were given arcades, with the west side occupied by St Paul's Church and the south side by the garden wall and market. The centre of the square was surrounded by wooden railings. Realising that the market could make him a profit, the fifth Earl obtained a charter from Charles II in 1670 and then let the management of it, including the collection of tolls from the traders, as a franchise, against £80 per year. In 1705 Bedford House was pulled down and the twenty-two shops with cellars built in 1677 against the garden wall of Bedford House were replaced by forty-eight outlets near the centre of the square, within the railings.

Another seventeenth-century development was Clare Market, built by the extremely rich John Holles, Earl of Clare, on land situated south of his house in Lincoln's Inn Fields. It was opened in 1656 as the New Market and was trading in meat, fish and other commodities. Market days were restricted to Tuesdays, Thursdays and Saturdays. In 1724 Daniel Defoe described it as one of the markets that had 'such numbers of buyers and such an infinite quantity of provisions of all sorts, flesh, fish and fowl, that, especially of the first, no city in the world can equal them'. Here were found twenty-six butchers (their outfits consisted of blue smocks with woollen aprons), who between them slaughtered 350 to 400 sheep per week, in the marketplace, stalls and cellars. Fifty to sixty bullocks (considerably more in winter) were killed in one area only, and the Jewish butchers had their own site where the animals could be slaughtered according to a 'ceremony prescribed by the laws of their religion' and where it was noticed that greater cleanliness was observed than elsewhere. We are told that the well-known actress Mrs Anne Bracegirdle 'was in the habit of going often into Clare market and giving money to the poor unemployed basket women'. Paxton & Whitfield of Jermyn Street started as cheesemongers in Clare Market in about 1740.

In 1664 Henry Jermyn erected St James's Market on a site close to present day Piccadilly Circus, for a thrice-weekly general market. Here Richard Wall started a sausage and pie business, which won him royal patronage and fame. In the same decade Berwick Street Market in Soho became established, followed in 1690 by Carnaby Market. In 1692 Lord Brooke was given a licence to open a meat market in Leather Lane.

The Earl of St Albans was granted the right to have a sheep and cattle market twice a week in the Haymarket and in 1663 he built a market house in the middle of the road on the stretch between Charles Street and Jermyn Street. This market was important in supplying the West End. In the early nineteenth century W. M. Edgar, later of the well-known Swan & Edgar store in Regent Street, had a haberdashery stall there, underneath which he slept at night.

In 1682 Sir Edward Hungerford had a market erected on the site of his burned-down mansion situated along the River Thames (now occupied by Charing Cross station). The market building, which may have been designed by Sir Christopher Wren, had a colonnade for shops, with rooms on the first floor. A new set of stairs was built down to the river, providing easy access both for the produce (some of it from the market gardens of Pimlico) and for the customers. It started as a fruit and vegetable market but found the competition with Covent Garden too great. Defoe mentions it as a meal market. Unfortunately it was never a success as its site was restricted.

The very popular and well-known Borough Market near London Bridge was founded in 1756 by an Act of Parliament. Claiming to be 'Great Britain's oldest food market', it is a charity and is administrated by sixteen trustees, who have to live in the local community. It covers 4½ acres. The free Borough Market Magazine *keeps customers informed of the latest developments.*

In the same year John Balch received a licence from Charles II to open a market at Spitalfields, close to the site of the medieval hospital of St Mary. This was an area which Defoe remembered as 'a field of grass with cows feeding on it', commenting on how it had become 'all town'. The market was opened in 1684 and in 1708 was described as a 'fine market for flesh, fowl and roots'. Three years later a great influx of French Huguenots into the area ensured that business thrived.

Close to Leicester Square, near present-day Little Newport Street, Newport

Tile panel in Hyde Park Corner underpass, representing the stable yard of Richard Tattersall, who set up his auction stables nearby.

In the early eighteenth century Defoe lists Whitechapel, Southwark, 'the Hay-Market-Street', Westminster, Bloomsbury and Smithfield, though the last had contracted as a result of room being needed for the increasing number of livestock that had to be accommodated.

Because hay is bulky and messy, the streets associated with it had to be wide, as was the case with the small hay markets established in the early sixteenth century in Broadway, Westminster, and Broadwick Street in Soho, both still wide thoroughfares. By the beginning of the eighteenth century these small markets were closed and all business was transferred to the Hay Market in Piccadilly. Soon 1,300 cartloads of hay passed through on Tuesdays, Thursdays and Saturdays, when trading took place. Although as far back as 1661 an inspector had been appointed, this seemed to have made no difference. Repeated requests to have the market moved elsewhere were ignored. Similarly the introduction of tolls in 1662, to be paid on all hay and straw 'brought into and standing for sale' – the income of which was to be used for street repairs – failed to stop the nuisance, aggravated by the Earl of St Albans's twice-weekly livestock market, already mentioned. The area became one of the filthiest in London and this continued until 1830, when an Act of Parliament addressed the 'great Obstruction to the Thoroughfare of the said Street and its Vicinity' and the 'Annoyance to the Inhabitants of the Street and its Vicinity' and moved the market to York Square, Clarence Gardens and Cumberland Market towards the north. In this same period the East End was served by the hay market in Whitechapel, established by Act of Parliament in 1708 and continuing until 1928.

As we have seen, corn markets, dealing in one of the most important staple foods for the population, were of prime importance and were to be found in a number of areas, chief amongst them Bear Quay and Queenhithe. As elsewhere in the country, a transformation started to take place in the corn trade when farmers, instead of bringing full loads of grain into the capital, started to leave samples with innkeepers who would take orders from interested parties on commission. Eventually corn agents took over and started selling from stands in different locations. This continued until a number of merchants raised enough money to commission a purpose-built corn exchange, which was opened in 1747 in Mark Lane (a corruption of Mart Lane, the former site of a medieval market). It was open to the sky and not roofed over until 1850.

The Corn Exchange, Mark Lane, c. 1835.

For the poor there were two important second-hand clothes markets, one at the Rag Fair in Rosemary Lane (mentioned by Alexander Pope in his poem 'The Dunciad', with a footnote explaining that the market was 'a place near the Tower where old clothes and frippery are sold') and the other at Petticoat Lane, (named, it is said, after the short (*petit*) coats worn by sixteenth-century men. In 1753 an anonymous visitor wrote of 'the dunghills of old shreds and patches for sale there'. Much that was sold was no more than tatters and there were those who made a living by searching for discarded and stolen clothes. Both markets had probably started in the seventeenth century but really came into their own in the eighteenth century as the continued growth of London's population meant that increasing numbers of people had to rely on their services.

In the East End, Club Row Market for live animals, no longer in existence, may have had its origins in the love of caged birds that the Huguenots brought with them as they settled in this area. Songbirds were trapped in Epping Forest and sold in tiny cages, to be hung outside people's windows, where they would sing.

The nineteenth century brought further population growth and a concomitant expansion of the capital. Though the City was still the centre of power, the area

Tile panel, entitled Whitechapel Hay Market 1788, *made in 1889 by Charles Evans & Company. (By kind permission of Lynn Pearson.)*

Wentworth Street Market, off Middlesex Street (formerly called Petticoat Lane), where in the past traders dealt in old clothes.

covered by it was now relatively small compared to London as a whole. Congestion on the roads led to the introduction of new and wider thoroughfares and in the process of redevelopment some markets were swept away, not to be replaced, as shops rather than market stalls became increasingly relied on.

In 1826–30 the by then run-down Fleet Market was pulled down to make way for Farringdon Street, and a new fruit and vegetable market was established, with a grand opening ceremony, involving wagons of vegetables pulled by horses decorated with ribbons. The market, a large paved courtyard, was famous for its watercress. Here street vendors, many of them children, bought their stock, which they divided into bunches. An eight-year-old girl, interviewed by Henry Mayhew, told him that she had to be at the market between 4 and 5 a.m., after which she would sell between 6 and 10 a.m., crying 'Creases, four bunches a penny, creases!' On a good day she might make 1s. but her average was 3d or 4d. The building of the Holborn Viaduct destroyed part of the market and eventually it closed down.

Also in the early nineteenth century the development of Waterloo Place and Regent Street spelled the end of St James's Market, and the site of the medieval meat market of Eastcheap was cleared for an improved approach to London Bridge – King William Street. In 1835 Honey Lane Market was swept away as the City of London School was built on its site (since further developed). Aldgate Meat Market went later in the century, as did Oxford Market. Newport Market was cleared for Charing Cross Road and Shaftesbury Avenue, and Newgate Market came to an end in 1869 as its functions were taken over by the Central Meat Markets, recently created on the site of the vacated livestock market at Smithfield. Towards the end of the nineteenth century Clare Market, now in a desperately poor area, had deteriorated. It was swept away between 1900 and 1905 and the London School of Economics now stands on part of the site.

Smithfield Market had remained a problem, even though already in 1756 the second Duke of Grafton had laid out the New Road (renamed Euston Road in 1857) so that cattle coming in from the west on their way to Smithfield could avoid Oxford Street and Holborn. Even so, there were complaints about the dust kicked up by the hooves of animals, which might also stray into shops and houses along the way.

The cattle market was still regulated by the old 'Statutes of Smithfield', laid down by the City authorities, who wanted to stay in control. However, as the volume of trade increased there were repeated arguments for its removal to a more suitable site. By 1834 it occupied an area of over 6 acres and was considered the largest livestock market in the world, with over fifteen hundred sheep pens and fifty for pigs. In 1846, 210,757 head of cattle, 1,518,510 sheep and 250,000 pigs were sold annually. The sales were done on commission, with fees of 4s. per ox and 8d per sheep. The City authorities received 1d in toll for an ox and charged 1s. for a score of sheep. The salesmen estimated the weight of the animals by eye and long experience meant that they were never far out. The sales were for cash and the bargain was struck by a shaking of the hands. There was no paperwork involved. It was estimated that every year £7 million changed hands this way. Market days were Mondays for fat cattle and sheep, Tuesdays, Thursdays and Saturdays for hay and straw, Fridays for cattle, sheep and milch cows, and from 2 p.m. for scrub horses and asses. Even in the nineteenth century animals were slaughtered in the market, with blood running down the street and offal clogging up the gutters. In *Oliver Twist* Charles Dickens describes the scene as the villain Sikes takes Oliver across Smithfield:

> It was market morning. The ground was covered, nearly ankle-deep, with filth and mire; a thick steam, perpetually rising from the reeking bodies of the cattle … hung heavily above. All the pens in the centre of the large area, and as many temporary pens as could be crowded into the vacant space, were filled with sheep; tied up to posts by the gutter were long lines of beasts and oxen, three or four deep. Countrymen, butchers, drovers, hawkers, boys, thieves, idlers, and vagabonds of every low grade, were mingled together in a mass; the whistling of drovers, the barking of dogs, the bellowing and plunging of oxen, the bleating of sheep, the grunting and squeaking of pigs, the cries of hawkers, the shouts, oaths and quarrelling on all sides; the ringing of bells and roar of voices, that issued from every public house; the crowding, pushing, driving, beating, whooping and yelling; the

Sunday bird fair off Brick Lane, London; twentieth century. (Museum of London/The Bridgeman Art Library.)

The Caledonian Market, 1902.

hideous and discordant din that resounded from every corner of the market; and the unwashed, unshaven, squalid and dirty figures constantly running to and fro, and bursting in and out of the throng; rendered it a stunning and bewildering scene...

In 1846 John Perkins tried to offer a solution by his purchase of 15 acres in Islington so that the cattle market could be moved away from the City, but his plans were obstructed by the authorities, afraid of losing control.

Finally, in 1855, the City Corporation bought a site of 30 acres in Copenhagen Fields. This was later opened by Prince Albert as the Metropolitan Cattle Market, where livestock was sold on Mondays, Thursdays and Fridays. On Saturdays the site was used for a general market, called the Caledonian Market because it was close to the Caledonian Road. A clock tower, still in existence, was placed on the site of Copenhagen House.

Leadenhall Market was rebuilt in 1881, to a design by the City architect, Sir Horace Jones. Constructed mostly of cast iron and glass, it consists of two covered roads and a dome over the crossing, held up by eight silvered dragons, representing the mythical wyverns of London. At this stage the poultry market was mostly wholesale, with live as well as dead animals for sale.

By the beginning of the nineteenth century Covent Garden had deteriorated into an unkempt area with fruit and vegetable dealers, as well as purveyors of other goods, occupying a variety of unsightly structures spread all over the square. These various traders constantly broke the rules and complained about the tolls that had to be paid. In order to assert his authority, the sixth Duke of Bedford appointed Charles Fowler to design a new market building, which, when built in 1830, consisted of a row of covered retail shops in the middle, with wholesale areas (which were open to the sky but had underground storage space) on either side. In an article dated 29 April 1848 the *Illustrated London News* described the market as 'the ever-open flower-show of London. In spring, summer, autumn or winter, the choicest treasures of the floral world are here collected; from the

The new livestock market in Islington.

Columbia Market, Bethnal Green. Financed by Angela Burdett-Coutts, it was opened by the Prince of Wales in 1869. It did not prove a success and was demolished in 1958.

conservatory, and the humble cottage-garden, flowers of all hues are gathered to grace the Covent-Garden colonnades.' Some years later the wholesalers petitioned the Duke for a roof over their areas and this was achieved with a glazed iron structure standing over the former open area, but not touching the original building.

Until 1850 Billingsgate fish market consisted of 'an open area dotted with low booths and sheds, with a range of wooden houses with a piazza in front on the west'. To improve on this, J. B. Bunning designed a purpose-built market hall in the 1850s but this soon proved inadequate and it was torn down in favour of a new building by Sir Horace Jones, the architect of the new Leadenhall Market. This handsome building, opened in 1877, combined utility inside with a decorative exterior, topped with golden dolphins and a fish weathervane. Yet even this proved inadequate and already in 1883 comments were made on 'the deficiencies of Billingsgate'.

Two of the eight silvered dragons, representing the mythical wyverns of London, upholding the dome of Leadenhall Market, built by Horace Jones in 1881.

A spectacular development happened along the Columbia Road in the East End. Here in 1869 the Prince of Wales opened the very grand Columbia Market, financed by the wealthy heiress Angela Burdett-Coutts. Costing more than £200,000, it had been designed by H. A. Darbyshire on a most lavish scale. The market hall was built in the Gothic style with a central clock tower, with bells playing a hymn every quarter of an hour. The quadrangle, it was reported in the *Illustrated London News*, measuring '14,000 superficial feet, was paved with blue granite, divided by lines of red granite into spaces 6 ft square, which are to be stations for costermongers'. Shops and fourteen apartments for city clerks were included in the complex, the main object of which was to clear traders, and the unhygienic messes they created, off the street. The project proved to be a failure, with costermongers unwilling to move, and the market closed within six months. Though Angela Burdett-Coutts made various attempts to reuse the buildings, first as a fish market, then as a meat market, followed by another attempt at fish selling, none of these was successful and in 1885 the market closed for good. It was demolished in 1958.

By the twentieth century what had started to be known as the West End had become the hub of retail enterprise, with many department stores vying for custom. In less central areas most streets had corner shops where everyday commodities were available. Yet markets did not disappear and even in the twenty-first century stalls, and the occasional barrow, can still be found in Berwick Street (Soho), Chalton Street (between Euston Station and the British Library), Brick Lane and Wentworth Street (Whitechapel), Electric Avenue (Brixton) and elsewhere. Portobello Market (Notting Hill) – 'London's liveliest street on Saturdays' – and the East End's Petticoat Lane (Middlesex Street) – 'the most famous of all London's street markets' – open on

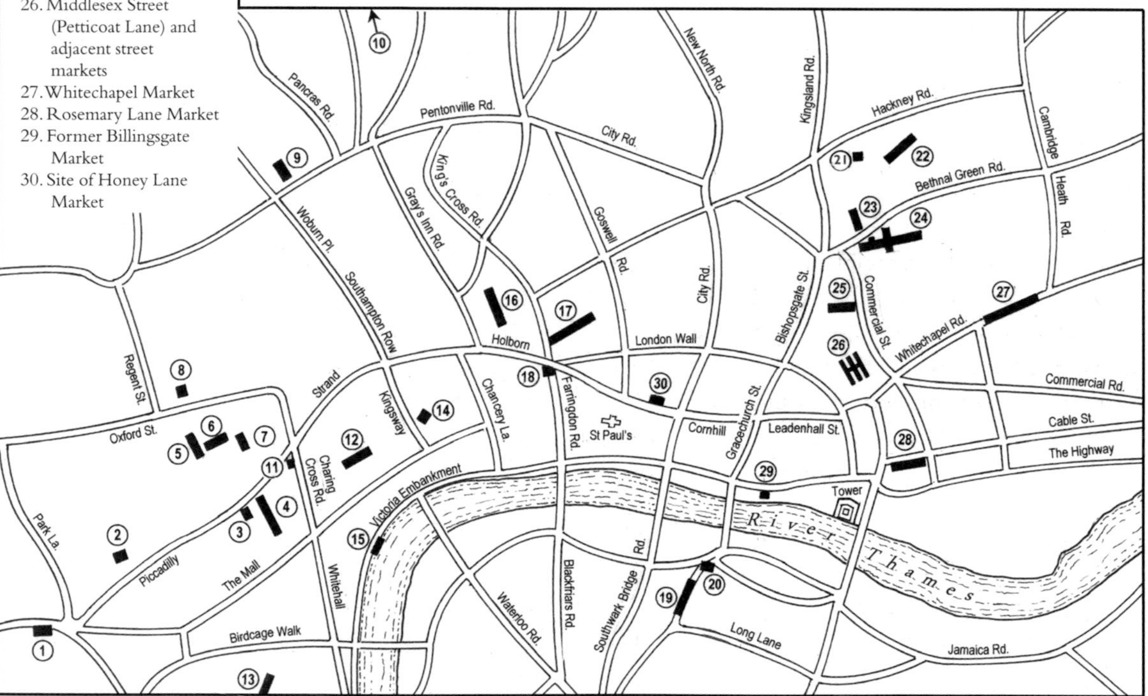

Sites of London markets in the post-medieval period.

1. Tattersall's
2. Shepherd Market
3. St. James's Market
4. Haymarket and the Earl of St Alban's Sheep and Cattle Market
5. Carnaby Market
6. Haymarket, Broadwick Street
7. Berwick Street Market
8. Oxford or Portland Market
9. Chalton Street Market
10. Metropolitan Cattle Market and the Caledonian Market
11. Newport Market
12. Covent Garden
13. Former Haymarket in Broadway
14. Clare Market
15. Hungerford Market
16. Leather Lane Market
17. Smithfield
18. Farringdon Fruit and Vegetable Market
19. Medieval market, Southwark High Street
20. Borough Market
21. Columbia Market
22. Columbia Road Flower Market (Sunday mornings only)
23. Club Row Market
24. Brick Lane Market
25. Old Spitalfields Market
26. Middlesex Street (Petticoat Lane) and adjacent street markets
27. Whitechapel Market
28. Rosemary Lane Market
29. Former Billingsgate Market
30. Site of Honey Lane Market

Billingsgate New Market, built in 1877.

Sundays, and are still thronged every week, as is a twenty-first-century addition in the former Truman's Brewery off Brick Lane.

In Covent Garden the fruit and flowers have disappeared, having moved to Nine Elms (Vauxhall), to be replaced by shops, restaurants and craft stalls, though barrows are still in evidence. In 1982, after nine hundred years at Billingsgate, the fishmongers moved to the Isle of Dogs, leaving a building that still graces the riverfront. The fruit and vegetable market of Spitalfields has also moved away from its earlier site, which now has shops and craft stalls. The only wholesale market left in the City is the London Central Markets at Smithfield, considered the oldest and largest dead meat market in Europe. Its enormous buildings, designed by Horace Jones, the City architect who also gave London the market buildings in Leadenhall and Billingsgate, still form a formidable presence. The Lord Mayor visits each of these markets during his year of office and is presented with a gift by each of them. The butchers usually offer three cuts of meat.

Smithfield Market is considered the oldest and largest dead meat market in Europe.

Outside the city there are no better examples than Brixton Market and the Borough Market (which has added a retail market – busiest on Saturdays but now also operating on Thursdays and Fridays – to its wholesale activities) south of the river, and Columbia Street Flower Market (Sunday mornings only) and Queen's Market ('the most ethnically diverse market for food, traders and shoppers') north of the river. All attract buyers from all over London and beyond.

CONCLUSION

MANY MARKETS have disappeared. It has been suggested that sterile supermarkets, shopping malls and 'shopping villages' have taken over from the less sanitised barrows. But market traders are hardy and they are fighting back, not least via organisations like the National Association of British Market Authorities (NABMA), which for many decades has represented local authority markets. Joined by the Association of Private Market Operators (APMO) in 2007, this society inspires its members to capture new business in innovative ways, disseminating ideas through its website, the publication of a magazine and regular meetings held in different parts of Britain. As a result in some areas special events have been organised by local traders and markets are being promoted as exciting places to visit. NABMA runs training courses for officers, offers legal advice, runs focus groups and has competitions for Best Market of the Year in three classes: indoor markets, street and outdoor markets, and specialist markets. It has direct access to the government through its All-Party Parliamentary Group on Markets. The National Market Traders' Federation also has its own magazine, in which matters of concern are discussed.

There are many thriving markets, providing a colourful shopping experience in towns and cities. Sometimes special bus services are laid on, with coaches given preferential treatment in the form of free parking and a complimentary lunch for drivers, and the organisers of coach parties also getting their rewards. Many towns still have indoor as well as outdoor markets, with the former usually open five or six days a week and the latter operating on specific days only. Bury (Lancashire) claims that its market is 'world famous'. Chesterfield (Derbyshire) has one of the biggest open-air markets in the country, whilst Leicester is said to have the largest indoor market in Europe (built in the 1970s), and Swansea the largest indoor market in Wales. Constructed in 1961, the latter is much admired for its glass roof. In contrast, shoppers in Tenbury Wells (Worcestershire) still flock to the small, pretty Round Market with its indoor and outdoor stalls, built in 1858 to give shelter to farmers' wives when it replaced the butter cross. Some markets combine the indoors with the outdoors, with permanent, lockable stalls under colourful awnings, grouped in the marketplace. Examples can be found in Norwich and Great Yarmouth (both in Norfolk).

New variations on an old theme can be found in the many specialist markets that take place all over the country, from continental and seasonal Christmas markets to farmers' markets, antiques and arts markets, as well as car-boot and table-top sales and the unique annual holly and mistletoe auctions at the end of November and the beginning of December in Tenbury Wells.

Even where markets have disappeared, visitors and local people alike are often reminded of their former existence by the layout of a town or the name of a street, pub, car park or housing estate. Smithfield Street in Oswestry (Shropshire) can be found near the former cattle market, now a car park. The Drovers' Restaurant in Llandovery (Carmarthenshire) and the Drovers' Arms in Rhewl (Denbighshire) remind us of the large herds of animals that once passed through these places.

OPPOSITE
Markets are here to stay. Newcastle-under-Lyme market (Staffordshire), 1999; oil on board, by Jiri Borsky. (Newcastle-under-Lyme Museum and Art Gallery. By kind permission of Jiri Borsky and the Newcastle-under-Lyme Museum and Art Gallery.)

The Round Market in Tenbury Wells (Worcestershire) was built in 1858 to give shelter to farmers' wives.

Horsefair in Deddington (Oxfordshire) gives notice of the trade that was carried out there and Old Market Square off the Columbia Road in East London marks the area where Angela Burdett-Coutts built her ill-fated market hall in 1869, replaced by blocks of flats in 1958. There are many Market Streets, Cheapsides and Smithfields. In Winslow (Buckinghamshire) Bell Walk, near the former cattle market, reminds of the auctioneer's bell that was rung to warn traders gathered in the nearby pub that business was about to begin.

Sometimes an artist's representation of, or allusion to, what has been lost can be found. As we have seen, many livestock markets have disappeared. In Beverley (Yorkshire) the supermarket now occupying part of the site vacated by the farmers and their animals displays a cast-metal relief depicting a pen crammed with sheep, surrounded by farmers. In a similar situation, a large store in Market Harborough (Leicestershire) has a mural made of bricks showing an auctioneer with a dog and different kinds of market produce.

In Festival Square, Oswestry (Shropshire), close to the former livestock market, a statue of a farmer with a ram can be found, and in London Fields, Hackney (London), a sculpture of flower sellers and sheep is said to mark the last resting place of drovers and their charges on their way to Smithfield. Another depiction of a drover (*porthmon* in Welsh) can be found in Llandovery (Carmarthenshire). Craven Arms (Shropshire) is reminded of its former claim to the 'largest sheep sale' in England by a sculpture showing rows of the animals on what could be described as the bare branches of a tree, walking dreamily into space.

The holly and mistletoe auctions in Tenbury Wells (Worcestershire) take place at the end of November and the beginning of December every year.

Pavement art includes a poem inscribed in the slabs outside the City Halls, the old Candleriggs Market (now Merchant Square) and the Fruit Market in Glasgow, including the lines:

EARTHY MUSHROOMS.
LETTUCE, ARE THEY CRISP, COOL,
ROLL THEM OUT. IF THE PEPPERS
ARE GLISTENING, GOOD.
BEDS OF CRESS, THEY'LL GO.
CRATED PINEAPPLES, FIERCE
AS LOBSTERS, WATCH THEM!

Both Andover (Hampshire) and Huntingdon (Cambridgeshire) commemorate the granting of their charters by King John in 1205, the former in a mosaic (which includes a reference to Weyhill Fair, 'the greatest fair in the kingdom', which used to be held nearby), the latter with an inscription within a ring of bricks in the Market Place. In addition to a colourful mural showing cattle and sheep under a tree in a field, to be found in the market area, Newton Abbot (Devon) also has an oval slab showing three farmers behind a fence looking at a sheep and her lamb, with the words 'THE MARKET 1220'. Amongst the various images found along the time-line displayed in the pavement at Doncaster (Yorkshire) are a depiction of the market cross of 1152 and the butter cross of 1752.

In the Market Place of St Neots (Cambridgeshire), which claims to be 'one of the largest in the country', bollards surrounding the Day Column (an elaborate cast-iron lamp-post supporting four lanterns, dating to 1822) have been cast in the shape of monks, reminding passers-by that the first market stalls were set up by the walls of the nearby priory, which received its market charter *c.* 1180.

Finally, in Monmouthshire the former market area of Chepstow (from *Ceap Stowe* or 'place of exchange') is enhanced with a wonderful combination of sculptures, lettering and reliefs, involving steps and seats to cope with the sloping site. There are reminders of the produce sold and the containers in which it was displayed and taken home, of the weights and measures that might be used, the animals brought for sale and the coins needed to pay. Pride in local produce is expressed by the words: 'Unlike the flabby fish in London sold/ A Chepstow salmon's worth his weight in gold.'

A shopping centre and new market hall in Lancaster are enhanced with a mural showing a rural scene including sheep and a sheepdog, letters spelling 'MARKET' dangling from meat hooks, coins set into the pavement, bollards in the shape of weights and the set of ancient measurements already mentioned.

The large number of markets that thrive do not look all that different from the images, in paintings and prints, of their earlier manifestations, though perhaps they are a little tidier and certainly more hygienic. It could be said that the Women's Institute members seen in many market towns represent the latest incarnation of the farmers' wives of earlier times selling their home-made produce. Market stalls are very similar to their medieval forerunners, and some merchandise, plants for

The sculpture of flower sellers and sheep in London Fields, Hackney (London), marking the site where drovers rested before making their way to Smithfield.

example, is still displayed on the ground. As in the past, traders – particularly those working in the open air – suffer in bad weather, though they do have the benefit of electric lighting on dark days. Problems with crime also do not seem to have changed much and traders still complain about pedlars or hawkers, described as a 'nightmare in summer resorts and at Christmas', unfairly taking away trade as they sell goods without a licence. There is even a modern equivalent of the stocks: the exposure of dishonest traders, photographs included, in the local and trade press. As is the case with traders, the experience of shoppers would be recognised by medieval customers, down to the language used to express satisfaction with a bargain that was really 'cheap'.

The relief in Beverley (Yorkshire) depicting the former cattle market on the site now occupied by a supermarket and car park.

FURTHER READING

Anderson, Janice. *Collins' Guide to the Markets and Fairs of Great Britain.* Collins, 1988.

Ayto, John, and Crofton, Ian. *Brewer's Britain and Ireland.* Weidenfeld & Nicolson, 2005.

Baverstock, Keith and Fiona. *Discovering Walks in Edinburgh.* Shire, 1973.

Bell, Colin and Rose. *City Fathers.* Penguin Books, 1972.

Bennett, Julian. *Towns in Roman Britain.* Shire, 2001.

Brown, Jonathan. *The English Market Town.* The Crowood Press, 1986.

Bruyn Andrews, C. (editor). *The Torrington Diaries.* Methuen, 1970.

Burke, Gerald. *Towns in the Making.* Edward Arnold, 1971.

Chamberlain, Russell. *The English Country Town.* Webb & Bower, 1983.

Chamberlain, Russell. *English Market Towns.* Book Club Associates by arrangement with Weidenfeld & Nicolson, 1985.

Chandler, John. *John Leland's Itinerary.* Sutton Publishing, 1993.

Clark, Peter. *Country Towns in Pre-industrial England.* Leicester University Press, 1981.

Clark, Peter, and Slack, Paul. *English Towns in Transition 1500–1700.* Oxford University Press, 1976.

Clifford, Sue, and King, Angela. *England in Particular.* Hodder & Stoughton, 2006.

Clifton-Taylor, Alec. *Six English Towns.* BBC, 1978.

Defoe, Daniel (edited by P. N. Furbank, W. R. Owens and A. J. Coulson). *A Tour Through the Whole Island of Great Britain.* Yale University Press, 1991.

Dickens, Charles. *The Adventures of Oliver Twist.*

Girouard, Mark. *The English Town.* Yale University Press, 1990.

Girouard, Mark. *Town and Country.* Yale University Press, 1992.

Godwin, Fay, and Toulson, Shirley. *The Drovers' Roads of Wales.* Whittet Books, 1987.

Graham, J. T. *Scales and Balances.* Shire, 2003.

Graham, J. T. *Weights and Measures.* Shire, 2003.

Haines, George H. *Discovering Crosses.* Shire, 1969.

Haldane, A, R. B. *The Drove Roads of Scotland.* Edinburgh University Press, 1971.

Hardy, Thomas. *The Mayor of Casterbridge.*

Hindle, Brian Paul. *Medieval Town Plans.* Shire, 1990.

Hindle, Paul. *Medieval Roads and Tracks.* Shire, 1998.

Kostov, Spiro. *The City Assembled.* Little, Brown, 1999.

Lloyd, David W. *The Making of English Towns.* Victor Gollancz, 1992.

Moore-Colyer, Richard. *Welsh Cattle Drovers.* Landmark Publishing, 2006.

Morris, Christopher (editor). *The Illustrated Journeys of Celia Fiennes.* Macdonald, 1882.

Morrison, Kathryn A. *English Shops and Shopping.* Yale University Press (in association with English Heritage), 2004.

Morton, H.V. *In Search of England.* Penguin Books, 1927.

Nicolson, Adam, and Morter, Peter. *Prospects of England.* Weidenfeld & Nicolson, 1989.

Platt, Colin. *The English Medieval Town*. Granada, 1979.

Ridley, Anthony. *Living in Cities*. Heinemann, 1971.

Rimmer, Alfred. *Ancient Streets and Homesteads of England*. Macmillan, 1877.

Royal Commission on the Ancient and Historical Monuments of Scotland. *Tolbooths and Town-Houses – Civic Architecture in Scotland to 1833*. The Stationery Office, 1996.

Schmiegen, James, and Carls, Kenneth. *The British Market Hall*. Yale University Press, 1999.

Stevenson, Maurice. *Weights and Measures of the City of Winchester*. Winchester Museums Service, n.d.

Toulson, Shirley. *Lost Trade Routes*. Shire, 1983.

Toulson, Shirley. *The Drovers*, 2005.

Wacher, J. S. *The Towns of Roman Britain*. Routledge, 1995.

LONDON

Archer, Ian; Barron, Caroline; and Harding, Vanessa (editors). *Hugh Alley's Caveat: The Markets of London in 1598*. London Topographical Society, 1988.

Clout, Hugh. *History of London*. Times Books, fourth edition 2004.

Forshaw, Alec, and Bergstrom, Theo. *Markets of London*. Penguin Books, 1983.

Gardner, Douglas. *The Covent Garden Guide*. Ernest Benn (in association with Edward Stanford), 1980.

Grant, Neil. *Village London Past and Present*. Bounty Books, 2004.

Hyde, Ralph. *Ward Maps of the City of London*. London Topographical Society, 1999.

Jonson, Ben. *Bartholomew Fair* (edited by G. R. Hibbard). A. & C. Black, 2001.

Masters, Betty R. *The Public Markets of the City of London Surveyed by William Leybourn in 1677*. London Topographical Society, 1974.

Mayhew, Henry (edited by Stanley Rubenstein). *The Street Trader's Lot*. Readers' Union, 1949.

Richardson, John. *The Annals of London*. Cassell, 2000.

Stow, John. *The Survey of London*. Everyman's Library, 1980.

Uncle Jonathan. *Walks in and around London*. Charles H. Kelly, 1889.

Weinreb, Ben, and Hibbert, Christopher. *The London Encyclopaedia*. Macmillan, 1983.

Whitfield, Peter. *London: A Life in Maps*. The British Library, 2006.

GENERAL

The Pevsner Architectural Guides: The Buildings of England, The Buildings of Scotland, The Buildings of Wales and The Buildings of Ireland. Various authors. Yale University Press. These four series of architectural guides, covering different parts of the British Isles, were started in 1951 by Nikolaus Pevsner and are continually updated.

The Victoria History of the Counties of England (series). Oxford University Press, 1903 onwards. These volumes, covering the history of individual counties, are usually available in local studies libraries.

INDEX

Page numbers in italic refer to illustrations